THE SOUTHERN UPLAND WAY

SCOTLAND'S COAST TO COAST TRAIL

D1350611

About the Author

Alan has trekked in over thirty countries within Europe, Asia, North and South America, Africa and Australasia, and for seventeen years led organised walking holidays in several European countries. A member of the British Outdoor Writers and Photographers Guild, he has written more than a dozen walking guidebooks, several on long-distance mountain routes in France. His longer solo walks include a Grand Traverse of the European Alps between Nice and Vienna (1510 miles), the Pilgrim's Trail from Le Puy to Santiago de Compostela (960 miles) and a Coast-to-Coast across the French Pyrenees (540 miles). A Munroist and erstwhile National Secretary and Long Distance Path Information Officer of the Long Distance Walkers Association, Alan now lives at the foot of the Moffat Hills in Scotland, in the heart of the Southern Uplands.

Alan's first encounter with the Southern Upland Way was in 1995, when he backpacked the full length of the trail. A decade later he repeated the complete route a second time, this time mainly using bed and breakfast and hotel accommodation, in order to research this guidebook. He has travelled extensively on foot in most areas of the Southern Uplands, having climbed all of the Donalds and most of the other hills above 500m in height, and traversed them from south to north in 2003 as part of his walk between Land's End and John o'Groats.

Other guidebooks by Alan Castle for Cicerone:

Tour of the Queyras (French & Italian Alps) – 1990 (new edition 2008)

The Robert Louis Stevenson Trail (Cévennes, France) – 1992 (new edition 2007)

Walks In Volcano Country (Auvergne and Velay, France) – 1992

Walking the French Gorges (Provence and the Ardèche) – 1993

The Brittany Coastal Path – 1995
Walking in the Ardennes – 1996
The River Rhine Trail – 1999
Walking in Bedfordshire – 2001
The John Muir Trail – 2004
Alan also wrote the first and second editions of The Corsican High Level Route and A Pyrenean Trail (GR 10)

THE SOUTHERN UPLAND WAY

SCOTLAND'S COAST TO COAST TRAIL

by

Alan Castle

2 POLICE SQUARE, MILNTHORPE, CUMBRIA LA7 7PY
www.cicerone.co.uk

First edition 2
ISBN-13: 978

© Alan Castle 2007

A catalogue record for this book is available from the British Library.

Photographs

Ordnance
Survey

Licence number PU100012932

This product includes mapping data licensed from Ordnance Survey with the permission of the Controller of Her Majesty's Stationery Office © Crown copyright 2002. All rights reserved.

For my mother (1913 – 2002)

Acknowledgements

I am particularly indebted to Andrew Case of **southernuplandway.com** for help with the accommodation logistics during my research along the Way, and to Richard Mearns, Dumfries & Galloway Council SUW Ranger, who provided much up-dated information on the route, especially on the various changes to the line of the SUW over recent years. I would also like to thank Mike Baker, Scottish Borders Council SUW Ranger, and Jude Allison of Dumfries & Galloway Tourist Board for information and support. Thanks go also to the various owners and staff of the hotels and bed and breakfast establishments who provided me with accommodation and meals, often at reduced prices, whilst I researched the Way, and in particular to the proprietors of the Plantings Inn, Castle Kennedy, the Butchach Bed & Breakfast, New Luce, House o' Hill Hotel, Bargrennan, Blackaddie House Hotel, Sanquhar, the Garage Bed & Breakfast, Wanlockhead and the Camping and Caravanning Club. Finally, a thank you to the Stair Estates for help given during my visit to Castle Kennedy Gardens.

I am grateful, as always, to my wife, Beryl Castle, for all her advice, support and encouragement during the planning, research and writing of this guidebook.

Advice to Readers

Readers are advised that while every effort is taken by the authors to ensure the accuracy of this guidebook, changes can occur which may affect the contents. It is advisable to check locally on transport, accommodation, shops, and so on, but even rights of way can be altered.

The publisher would welcome notes of any such changes.

Front cover: Loch of the Lowes and St Mary's Loch (Stage 8)

CONTENTS

Where the pools are bright and deep,
Where the grey trout lies asleep,
Up the river and o'er the lea,
That's the way for Billy and me.

Where the blackbird sings the latest,
Where the hawthorn blooms the sweetest,
Where the nestlings chirp and flee,
That's the way for Billy and me.

James Hogg (1770–1835)
The Ettrick Shepherd

Over the hill to Away!

Tom Pow, Galloway poet

Southern Upland Way – Summary of Stages

		Distance	
		miles	km
Stage 1	Portpatrick to Castle Kennedy	13.4	21.6
Stage 2	Castle Kennedy to New Luce	8.9[1]	14.3
Stage 3	New Luce to Bargrennan	17.8[1]	28.6
Stage 4	Bargrennan to St John's Town of Dalry	24.3	39.1
Stage 5	St John's Town of Dalry to Sanquhar	26.7	43.0
Stage 6	Sanquhar to Wanlockhead	7.4	11.9
Stage 7	Wanlockhead to Beattock (Moffat)	20.5[2]	33.0
Stage 8	Beattock (Moffat) to Tibbie Shiels (St Mary's Loch)	20.9[2]	33.6
Stage 9	Tibbie Shiels (St Mary's Loch) to Traquair (Innerleithin)	12.0[3]	19.3
Stage 10	Traquair (Innerleithin) to Melrose	17.3[3]	27.8
Stage 11	Melrose to Lauder	10.2	16.4
Stage 12	Lauder to Longformacus	15.4	24.8
Stage 13	Longformacus to Cockburnspath	17.2	27.7
Total	**Portpatrick to Cockburnspath**	**212**	**341**

[1] This distance is to/from a point on the SUW at grid reference NX192650 on a minor road ENE of New Luce. New Luce is an additional mile (1.6km) from here off-route of the SUW.

[2] This distance is to/from Beattock on the SUW. Moffat is an additional 1.3 miles (2.1km) from Beattock off-route of the SUW.

[3] This distance is to/from Traquair on the SUW. Innerleithen is an additional 1.3 miles (2.1km) from Traquair off-route of the SUW.

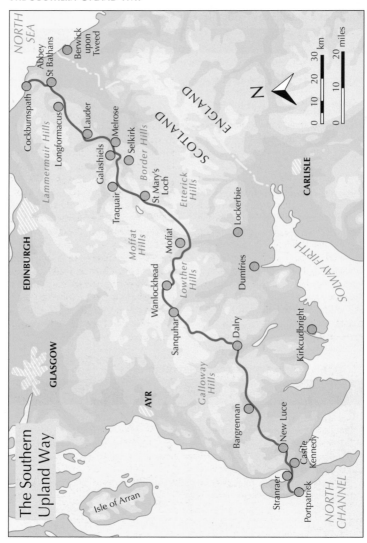

The Southern Upland Way

NORTH SEA

Abbey
St Bathans
Berwick
upon Tweed
Cockburnspath
Longformacus
Lammermuir Hills
Lauder
Melrose
Galashiels
Selkirk
Border Hills
Traquair
St Mary's Loch
Etterick Hills
SCOTLAND
ENGLAND
Lockerbie
CARLISLE
Moffat Hills
Moffat
Lower Hills
Wanlockhead
Dumfries
SOLWAY FIRTH
Sanquhar
Dalry
Kirkcudbright
EDINBURGH
GLASGOW
Galloway Hills
Bargrennan
New Luce
AYR
Castle
Kennedy
Stranraer
Portpatrick
Isle of Arran
NORTH CHANNEL

INTRODUCTION

THE SOUTHERN UPLAND WAY

The best long-distance walking trails have two characteristics that make them great: a succession of dramatic landscapes coupled with a broad selection of interesting places to visit along the way. The Southern Upland Way (SUW), Scotland's Coast to Coast Walk, scores highly on both. As the Way cuts across the grain of the country many different landscapes are unveiled, coastal cliffs, high moorland, rolling hills, remote mountains, forests, lochs, mountain streams, majestic rivers and sylvan valleys abounding in wildlife. The SUW passes through regions that are exceedingly rich in archaeological and historical associations, from prehistoric standing stones to monuments commemorating the Killing Times of the 17th-century Covenanters. There are formal gardens and stately homes to visit en route as well as some of the more elegant towns of Dumfries & Galloway and the Borders, such as Moffat and Melrose, the latter with its famous abbey – so many places of interest to stimulate and delight the visitor. Long-distance walking is all about exploring new territory and at a pace where it can be fully savoured. The Southern Uplands of Scotland are probably the least visited area of Britain, and it is likely that most

The border fence on the SUW between Dumfries & Galloway and the Borders (Stage 8)

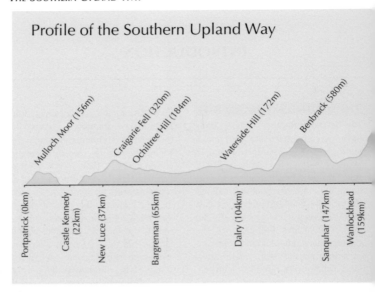

Profile of the Southern Upland Way

Mulloch Moor (156m)
Craigairie Fell (320m)
Ochiltree Hill (184m)
Waterside Hill (172m)
Benbrack (580m)

Portpatrick (0km)
Castle Kennedy (22km)
New Luce (37km)
Bargrennan (65km)
Dalry (104km)
Sanquhar (147km)
Wanlockhead (159km)

walkers who venture out from Portpatrick on the west coast will be discovering an area that for them was hitherto unknown: they will be pleasantly surprised. The SUW has it all! If you choose this trail for your annual walking holiday then you will certainly not be disappointed.

The 212 mile (341km) long SUW starts out from the west coast of Scotland at the picturesque old harbour of Portpatrick and, after a few kilometres following the dramatic cliff tops north of here, swings inland to begin its long journey eastward, firstly across the narrow Rhins peninsula. Kennedy Gardens, ablaze with rhododendrons and azaleas in season, is

passed en route for New Luce, where the story of the Covenanters and the Killing Times starts to unfold. A crossing of the remote and beautiful Galloway Hills follows, through Bargrennan and on to dramatic Loch Trool, site of one of Robert the Bruce's victories over the English in 1307. After Clatteringshaws Loch comes friendly St John's Town of Dalry, from where walkers set out on the longest section of the Way, across the hills to Sanquhar, where Britain's oldest post office dating from 1763 will be seen in the High Street. Wanlochhead, at 425m (1394ft) is Britain's highest village and home to the Museum of Scottish Lead Mining, where time may

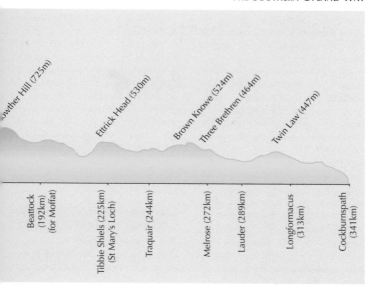

...wther Hill (725m)   Ettrick Head (530m)   Brown Knowe (524m)   Three Brethren (464m)   Twin Law (447m)

Beattock (192km) (for Moffat)   Tibbie Shiels (225km) (St Mary's Loch)   Traquair (244km)   Melrose (272km)   Lauder (289km)   Longformacus (313km)   Cockburnspath (341km)

be taken off from the route to visit an old lead mine. The SUW now climbs to its highest point at 720m (2362ft) on the Lowther Hills before dropping down to the Evan and Annandale Valleys, where a full day off from the route could be well spent exploring Moffat and its beautiful environs.

A crossing of the Ettrick Hills leads out of Dumfries & Galloway and into the Scottish Borders, first with a visit to Tibbie Shiels, one of the most famous old hostelries in Scotland. A walk along the shores of St Mary's Loch, southern Scotland's longest, and haunt of James Hogg, the Ettrick Shepherd, one of Scotland's celebrated poets, leads on to Traquair

with its stately home which has strong associations with the Jacobites. An ancient drove road takes the SUW to the tranquil River Tweed, beloved of anglers, and on to Melrose, which with its ancient abbey ruins, formal gardens and Walter Scott associations is another place where first time visitors may wish to linger a while. The triplet of the Eildon Hills dominates the landscape hereabouts as the walk continues north-eastwards to reach 'Royal' Lauder, where Thirlestane Castle and Gardens may be visited. A long crossing of the wild and lonely Lammermuir Hills leads to the pretty village of Longformacus, after which a more gentle landscape, rich arable

11

countryside, leads to a final section along the cliffs of the east coast and into Cockburnspath, the eastern terminus of the SUW.

The SUW traverses most of the major habitat types found in southern Scotland, including coastal cliffs, open moorland, hill and mountain, farmland, parkland, deciduous and coniferous woodland, riverbanks and lochsides. The wildlife associated with these habitats will be seen at any time of the year, but spring when the birds are in full song and when the wild flowers are at their best, is particularly rewarding for nature lovers.

One false impression of the SUW, Scotland's longest National Trail, needs to be dispelled. Some people seem to believe that there are huge tracts of the trail through massive forestry plantations of sitka spruce. It is true, alas, that there are far too many forestry plantations in southern Scotland and the SUW certainly does pass through several of them. BUT, by far the majority of the route is outside these forests and on open hillside or in pleasant rural valleys. For example, the last 90km (56 miles) of the Way from Minch Moor east of Traquair to Cockburnspath on the coast is devoid of any large plantations, and the first two stages of the SUW in the west from Portpatrick to New Luce, a distance of around 25 miles, is more or less free of forestry. Several other large areas of hillside on the SUW are also in open country. Of particular note is the superb high-level section

from Wanlockhead over the Lowthers to Overfingland.

Hopefully by now your appetite for the SUW has been well and truly whetted. So you now want to walk the SUW, but how do you realise your dream? The Introductory sections that follow will help you in planning and arriving at the start of the walk, Portpatrick, and from there the Trail Guide should safely guide you day-by-day on the SUW 'Over the hill to Away!'

WHICH WAY TO GO: WEST TO EAST OR EAST TO WEST?

The Southern Upland Way can, of course, be walked in either direction. Those who decide to tackle all or a major part of the Trail, rather than ramblers using the SUW as part of day walks, need to make a decision as to which direction to head, either north-east from Portpatrick or south-west from Cockburnspath. All things being equal (and they often aren't because of personal circumstances, where you live, convenience of travel, arrangements with friends, etc) a west to east traverse is the direction of choice, as the route is described in this guide. The reason for this is quite simple and should be well appreciated by all those living in these temperate isles: the predominant winds across the country are south-westerlies. The depressions that come all too frequently across the Atlantic bring moisture-laden air from the south-

First SUW signpost – Portpatrick (Stage 1)

SOUTHERN UPLAND WAY

west and dump much of it across our mountains, hills and moors. So the chances are that if you walk from Portpatrick to Cockburnspath you will have the wind, and hence any unpleasant weather, at your back all the way. However, if you happen to be unlucky enough to choose a period when a bitterly cold north-easterly is blowing, not uncommon particularly in the winter months, then you may have reason to curse both my advice and your decision. But may the sun always be shining! From a scenic point of view the views are equally fine if the Trail is walked in either direction, so the only real consideration is the most likely direction of the wind and weather.

WHAT TIME OF YEAR TO WALK THE TRAIL?

Day walkers can use the SUW at any time of the year, although during the winter months on the upland sections of the Trail, walkers will need the usual winter hillwalking gear, together with the appropriate experience. When the hills are plastered in snow and ice then crampons and ice axes must be carried. The Southern Uplands may not be the Highlands of the North, but the landscape here is often nevertheless rough and unforgiving, and once off the route of the SUW then few paths and fewer sign-posts are the norm.

Long-distance walkers tackling all or major sections of the route would be

13

Castle Kennedy House and Gardens (Stage 2)

wise to confine their activities to the spring, summer or autumn months, from April to October, when the days are longer and the weather conditions (usually!) less severe. Only the hardiest, suitably experienced backpackers should consider walking the SUW in winter. An appreciable amount of the accommodation and other facilities that serve the way will be closed from November to March, so winter hikers have little alternative than to backpack and camp wild for several nights. For a winter crossing it is essential to be fully equipped and experienced enough to cope with short daylength, long, cold and dark winter nights, snow and ice on the route, and winter storms. Several of the long cross-country stages between towns and villages cannot be completed in the daylight available in a winter's day. Nevertheless a winter SUW comple-

tion would make for a very special and magical experience for well-equipped and experienced backpackers, but would be way beyond the 'comfort level' of most ramblers.

Summer has the advantage of generally warmer days, but as this is the period when the majority of people take their holidays there will be more competition for the available bed space in the area. Those who prefer solitude in the hills, moors and forests should not dismiss the main summer holiday time period as neither Dumfries & Galloway nor the Borders receive the number of walking visitors that often overcrowd the Lake District, Yorkshire Dales and other areas south of the border. The Southern Uplands offer one of the few areas in these densely populated islands to get far away from the madding crowd at any time of the year.

Spring and autumn are the seasons of choice. High pressure is perhaps more common during the Spring in Scotland, and days during May and June often (but not always!) present ideal walking conditions, bright, sunny and not overly warm. The general freshness and rebirth of life is stimulating during springtime and flower displays are a particular joy. A visit to the Kennedy Gardens (See Stage 2) passed at the western end of the SUW can be highly recommended at this time of year.

Autumn is a charming time of the year in southern Scotland, with its mellow colours and general feeling of seasonal contentment. The heather moorland is a blaze of purple, and the landscape is at its driest of the year after the warmth of the summer sun before the winter rains arrive. The romantic roar of stags can sometimes be heard during the annual rutting season in October. Accommodation tends to be less fully booked than in July and August, and days in early autumn are still of an adequate length for walking relatively long distances.

WAYS OF TACKLING THE SUW

For a few the challenge will be to walk the Southern Upland Way from coast to coast across Scotland as a continuous walk. It forms the basis of a superb walking holiday of about two weeks' duration. There is the choice of staying each night in a hotel, B&B establishment or hostel, carrying the minimum of equipment (but always taking sufficient warm and waterproof gear) or backpacking the route, carrying tent, food and cooking equipment. Obviously the advantage of the latter method is that idyllic camps can be made on several nights, and it removes the need to complete a full stage each day in order to reach accommodation, but of course the down side is carrying all the extra weight.

If you do not have the time available or the energy to walk the entire SUW as one expedition, then break it down into two or more sections. The best point to split the route in two is at Beattock/Moffat at the end of Stage 7, where there is good motorway (M74) access. The western half of the SUW could be walked from the west coast at Portpatrick to the Moffat area from where bus transport is readily available north towards Glasgow and Edinburgh or south to Lockerbie and Carlisle, from where transport connections home are plentiful. The western half of the SUW will take approximately a week to accomplish, but longer if time is spent at the various places of interest along the route, always the recommended way to walk a long-distance trail. At a later date return to Moffat/Beattock to walk the eastern half of the Way, soon leaving Dumfries & Galloway and crossing the entire Borders region to the North Sea on the east coast.

Splitting the SUW into smaller sections is generally not so convenient, because of public transport limitations, but it is certainly feasible in several areas with a little research and planning (see Appendix 3). More flexibility is obviously possible if relatives or friends can be persuaded to drive you to the start and/or pick you up at the end of your selected stage.

Those walking the entire route, whether in one go or in several major sections, are urged not to rush through this marvellous country. There is much to see and delight the visitor here. Remember that you are on holiday, not on a gruelling assault course. Relax and enjoy the area, particularly if it is your first visit. There are several possibilities along the route to take off a half-day, a full day or even several days to visit a place of interest, public garden, museum or the like, or for the compulsive walker to enjoy some of the first-rate hill walking on offer in the area. This

guidebook provides several ideas for breaks from the route of this sort, and the tourist offices on or near the SUW will doubtless provide other information and inspiration.

Those people living in southern and central Scotland and in northern England could walk the SUW in its entirety, but as separate day walks over as long or as concentrated a time period as desired. There are basically three ways of achieving this: use just one of these options throughout your 'campaign' or a mixture of all three.

1. Walk one section at a time in a 'there and back' manner. Drive or take public transport to the start of the Trail. Walk along the SUW to a village, town or point on a road where a car can be parked or public transport taken at a later date. Walk back along the SUW to your starting point. On your

The countryside near Lauder (Stage 11)

second visit drive or take public transport to the point you reached at the end of the first day of the Trail. Repeat this technique for as long as it takes to walk the whole of the SUW.

There are problems using this technique to walk the SUW, as in several areas the stages between roads where a car can be parked or transport obtained are often too long to allow for this 'there and back' approach, except for the fittest and faster walkers or runners. Sometimes roads will be crossed where it is unsuitable to park a car safely and responsibly without obstructing the road for other users, and considerable detours on foot would have to be made to find a suitable place to park a vehicle.

2. Plan to walk sections of the route with friends taking two cars. Park one car at the end of the section you intend to walk and drive together to the start of your day walk leaving the second car here. On reaching the end of your walk and arriving at the first car, drive back in this to pick up the car waiting for you at your day's starting point. A variation of this is to split the group into two, one parking a car at one end of the section and the other at the other end and each group walking in opposite directions. Swap car keys on meeting halfway through your day. This can only go wrong if one or both

groups stray from the line of the SUW! Bear in mind that reception for mobile phones is often poor in many of the areas through which the SUW passes. A safer option is for each driver to carry keys for the other car.

3. Use the SUW as just part of a large number of circular walks back to a parked car or place where public transport can be obtained. Continue these 'filling in the blanks' in the Trail until eventually the entire route has been covered.

It is not necessary, obviously, to use any of these techniques to walk the Way sequentially, from east to west or from west to east. Simply walk stages in any order as takes your fancy or is the most convenient.

Of course if you have no desire to walk the entire length of the SUW you can still enjoy sections of the Way on day walks using any or a combination of these techniques. The SUW is certainly not the sole preserve of the long-distance walker. Not everyone will have the ambition to walk every foot of the Way, but still the SUW offers a good, well waymarked walking route through some wonderful countryside and can be used in part by all types of walkers, from those content with a leisurely stroll of a mile or two to committed long-distance and hill walkers. For many the SUW will be used for just part of a day walk or longer

17

Southern Upland sheep

expedition across the Southern Uplands. Hillwalkers will often find that the Way forms convenient and easy access routes into remote hill country and after a hard day on the pathless tops often provides an undemanding and relatively fast route of return back to the car and civilisation.

Finally, give a thought to the idea of combining the SUW with one of the other long-distance paths in southern Scotland. A week long holiday in south-west Scotland could be had by walking the SUW from Portpatrick to New Luce, then south into the Machars to Whithorn along the Whithorn Pilgrim Way. A companion trip to this could be a week or ten days in the Borders and Northumbria along the SUW from

Moffat to Melrose, from where St Cuthbert's Way will lead you to Lindisfarne, Holy Island. The SUW also connects with the excellent Borders Abbeys Way at Melrose and the two trails combined would also make a worthwhile walking holiday.

LUGGAGE TRANSPORT AND DROP-OFF/PICK-UP SERVICES

Some commercial companies (see Appendix 3) operate luggage support services, whereby luggage is transferred from B&B/hotel establishments to the next one that has been booked further along the Way, so that only a small daysac need be carried. Those who think that they are incapable of leaving heavy luxuries at home should strongly consider use of these services. But one word of warning: always carry with you the essentials of adequate warm and waterproof clothing, first aid kit and any necessary medicines, and sufficient food and drink.

Some companies offer vehicle backup services, which are a very important consideration for walkers who would find the long distances of some of the stages of the SUW (particularly Stages 4, 5, 7 and 8) too demanding. By using these pick-up/drop down services the walker is able to divide the longer stages into more manageable day sections, but still spend each night in comfortable accommodation. See under the relevant Stages in the trail description for more details.

ACCOMMODATION ALONG THE SUW

At the end of each of the thirteen stages of the SUW described in this guide-book accommodation is available in the form of B&B establishments and/or hotels. There is plentiful choice in some of these locations, such as in Moffat, Galashiels, Melrose, less so in others, and just a few places where accommodation is more limited, such as at Bargrennan at the end of Stage 3. Four youth hostels serve the SUW. Wanlockhead Hostel (end of stage 6) and Melrose YH (end of stage 10) lie very close to the route, and two further hostels can be reached by short

detours from the Way, at Kendoon YH (Stage 5) and at Broadmeadows (Stage 10). Sometimes more choice is available a little off-route by walking or taking a taxi (or even sometimes, though rarely, a bus) to a nearby larger town; for example there is more accommodation available in Stranraer than in Castle Kennedy at the end of Stage 1. Some B&B owners will pick up SUW walkers by car if the B&B is a little off-route and will return them to the SUW the next morning.

It is strongly recommended that accommodation is booked for each night, particularly if there are more that two in your party, and if you are planning to walk in the height of the summer season or at bank holidays (remember that some bank holidays are different in Scotland from those in England – it is best to check on this before setting out). Each year an official SUW Accommodation Guide is produced by the SUW Ranger Services. This is available free of charge from local Tourist Information Centres (see Appendix 3), the staff of which will also provide more information on accommodation possibilities and book accommodation if required. The Accommodation Guide contains details of hotel, B&B, hostel, campsite and self-catering accommodation on or in the vicinity of the SUW, although some establishments listed are a considerable distance off-route. Also up-to-date information is available on the relevant websites, in particular

19

Brattleburn Bothy (Stage 7)

www.southernuplandway.com and www.dumgal.gov.uk/southernuplandway.

There are campsites with facilities on or close to the SUW at Portpatrick (Stage 1), Bargrennan (Glentrool Holiday Park – Stage 3), Sanquhar (Stage 5), Beattock (Craigielands – Stage 7), Moffat (Stage 7), Innerleithen (Stage 9) and Lauder (Thirlestane Campsite – Stage 11/12). Tibbie Shiels Inn (Stage 8) normally allows camping on their land, usually provided that a meal is taken in the hostelry, and 'no facilities' camping is normally available in Dalry (Stage 4). Note that Caldons Campsite, Loch Trool (Stage 4) is now permanently closed. Details of other places where there are campsites with facilities, or where it is permitted to camp are usually given in the SUW Accommodation Guide (see above).

Fully equipped backpackers are free to camp wild, provided they do so responsibly and well away from any habitation. The only real requirement is that you stay for one night only (unless the situation is an emergency) and that you leave no evidence whatsoever of your passing. Even if a tent is carried it is a good idea to make full use of the bothies provided along the Way (see Appendix 1).

Some details of where to expect supermarkets and other grocer shops, as well as cafés, restaurants and pubs are given in the relevant sections of the Trail Guide, but do remember that establishments do close and new ones open over time. For more up-to-date information see the annual SUW Accommodation Guide (see above) and contact the local Tourist Information Offices (see Appendix 3).

GETTING TO AND FROM THE SUW

Journey to Portpatrick

Train and long-distance coach services operate several times a day to Stranraer (Port Rodie) to link with the ferry to Belfast. An alternative is to take a train or long-distance coach to Dumfries, the county town of Dumfries & Galloway, and from there travel westwards by the local bus services, which are generally good. If taking the latter option catch bus number 500 from the bus shelter on Whitesands, alongside the River Nith in the centre of Dumfries. The journey time to Stranraer is about 2¼ hours. Opposite the point where this bus stops in Stranraer at Port Rodie (Harbour Street) will be found the bus stop shelter for the bus to Portpatrick (20 minutes journey). To make this bus journey from Dumfries to Portpatrick be sure to purchase a D&G 'Discoverer' ticket from the bus driver in Dumfries. This ticket can be used on both sections of the journey – from Dumfries to Stranraer and from Stranraer to Portpatrick, provided the complete journey is undertaken during one day. A Discoverer ticket is cheaper than the two separate fares.

There is plenty of accommodation in Dumfries (contact the Dumfries Tourist Information Centre, which is situated in Whitesands – open all year). One possibility is to travel from your home to Dumfries, spend a night there (take time to visit the Robert Burn's Centre, his house, mausoleum, etc) in a hotel or B&B, and take a bus the next morning to Stranraer. At the time of writing there is a No. 500 bus at 9.20am (Monday to Saturday) from Whitesands in Dumfries, arriving in Stranraer at 11.36am, with a connection to Portpatrick at 12.01pm, arriving at 12.23pm. This is most convenient for those wishing to start the SUW immediately on arrival at Portpatrick (or after lunch) as the first section to Castle Kennedy is only a half-day walk. However, to leave without spending some time in the delightful little coastal town of Portpatrick would be sacrilege.

Access to Portpatrick by private transport is via the A75, which leaves the A74/M74 north of Carlisle. From Stranraer take the A77 or a minor road across the Rhins to Portpatrick.

Journey from Cockburnspath

Local buses from Cockburnspath link with services north to Dunbar and Edinburgh and south to Berwick-on-Tweed and Newcastle. Those with private transport have the nearby A1 to take them to destinations both south and north.

Moffat

Those thinking of terminating their walk at the halfway stage in Moffat, or starting the eastern section of the Way from there, will find generally good public transport connections. There are several buses a day from Moffat to

Lockerbie and Carlisle and to Glasgow and Edinburgh. The nearest train station for the main line service south and north is at Lockerbie, 16 miles to the south of Moffat.

If driving to Moffat the town is situated just a mile from Junction 15 off the M74 motorway.

PLANNING: WHAT TO DO BEFORE YOU LEAVE HOME

If you have never undertaken a long-distance trail as a continuous walking holiday before, then a few hints at the planning stage may come in useful. The following checklist may be of assistance.

1. Book any accommodation that is required well in advance.
2. Check out all your travel arrangements, with timetables and fares for getting to the start of the Trail *and* getting home after you have finished the walk. Book if necessary.
3. Baggage Transfer. If using a commercial organisation to transport your luggage from accommodation address along the Trail (see Appendix 3), book this service well before you leave home.
4. Vehicle Support. If using a commercial organisation for vehicle support (particularly useful to overcome the problems associated with the long sections between Bargrennan, Dalry and Sanquhar), book this service well in advance.
5. Purchase all the equipment required well before the time you intend to set out for the walk. This is particularly important for boots, which must be well 'broken in' before using them on the SUW. If backpacking, make sure that you try out your equipment before your first night on the Trail to spot any possible flaws or problems associated with its use.
6. Training Walks. If you have not undertaken much walking throughout the previous year then it is essential that you take several long walks in the preceding couple of months or so before your big walk. Moreover, make sure that you carry on at least some of these walks the sort of weights in rucksac or backpack that you will be carrying on the SUW.
7. Pack your rucksac/backpack several days before you leave home to ensure that all your equipment fits well in the sac. Go through a checklist of essential items to be taken, remove any unnecessary items (apart from perhaps one or two lightweight luxuries), repack and carry the pack on a few short walks to ensure that it sits comfortably on the back and hips and that all is well. Make any necessary adjustments *before* you leave home.
8. Ensure that you have enough cash with you for either the

The River Tweed from Yair Bridge (Stage 10)

whole trip or until you can be certain of easily acquiring more.

9. On the first day of your holiday leave early for the train or bus station to avoid missing your transport which could put all your arrangements and accommodation reservations in jeopardy.

10. Start the walk and relax – all should now go like clockwork – just enjoy the walk!

EQUIPMENT

There are several suitable primers available these days with plentiful advice on equipment for various types of walking activities, and many glossy manufacturer's brochures detail all manner of high tech hiking equipment, so newcomers to walking are advised to consult these before setting out on the SUW.

But one point is worth emphasising here. Nothing more spoils a walking expedition than carrying a large, very heavy rucsac, particularly one containing lots of unnecessary equipment. The author is often amazed at the quantity of equipment that some people carry even on modest excursions. Assemble your equipment and then go through it carefully to see what may safely be left behind. If making use of B&B and hotel accommodation it should not be necessary to carry more than 15–20lbs, even including

23

food and drink. Backpackers should aim for under 30lbs and certainly never more than 35lbs on a route of this nature, where food is available at least every few days. The main things to consider when packing are to include

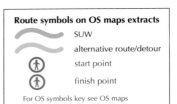

Route symbols on OS maps extracts

SUW

alternative route/detour

start point

finish point

For OS symbols key see OS maps

1. Good boots and sufficient cloth-
    ing plus emergency blanket to
    keep you warm, dry and safe,
2. Maps, guidebook, compass,
    torch, whistle,
3. A small first aid kit plus any per-
    sonal medicines,
4. A small washing kit (not a huge
    soap bag and no towel if using
    B&B or hotel accommodation),
5. Sufficient food and drink, includ-
    ing emergency food.

Most other items will be superfluous. My luxuries consist only of a camera and a small exercise book to be used as a travel journal. Backpackers will also need a good lightweight tent, sleeping bag, insulating mat, cooking stove, utensils, fuel and lightweight travel towel.

MAPS

This guidebook contains Ordnance Survey Landranger (1:50,000) mapping of the entire SUW with the route of the Trail clearly overlaid. Provided no serious navigational errors occur en route, nor long detours from the Way are envisaged, then in theory this is the only mapping

that is required to walk the Trail. However, many walkers will want to carry some general maps of the area with them, as these are useful for a number of reasons. When you reach one of the many viewpoints along the SUW you will see other distant hills and ranges, villages and small towns, and a whole topography of land and seascape. What are those villages, those hills, that coastline? Unless you have a detailed knowledge of the area, or are walking with a local guide, then the answers to these and other similar questions can only be answered by reference to a good map. Sometimes it will be necessary to divert from the actual line of the Way to secure a night's accommodation. Several places of interest are varying distances from the route, from a few hundred yards to several miles, and in order to plot the shortest or most inter-esting route to them and back onto the Trail, a map will be invaluable. So you must make a decision whether or not to carry other maps with you when walking the SUW.

If it is decided to carry other maps, then the decision must also be made as to which maps to purchase (or borrow

St Mary's Loch and the Loch of the Lowes seen from the upper reaches of Ox Cleuch (detour from Stage 8)

from a public library if desired). The decision is not an easy one to make as the route, heading generally north-eastwards across the southern half of Scotland cuts across a considerable number of Ordnance Survey map sheets. So if OS maps at either 1:50,000 scale or at 1:25,000 scale are to taken then there will firstly be a fairly considerable financial outlay in buying the maps, and then the extra weight and bulk of the maps will have to be tolerated whilst on the walk. A possible solution to these mapping problems is to use the very adequate OS maps of the route contained in this guidebook for actually walking the Trail, but also purchase a small scale map of the whole area, such as the OS's 1:250,000 scale map of Southern Scotland and Northumberland. The latter will be useful in overall planning before you leave home, but also can be used to identify distant features in a view and to provide an overview of the whole area through which you are passing. This map of course will have severe limitations if you intend to make detailed detours on foot for some distance from the route, although for relatively short on-foot diversions, the maps in this book will be more than adequate.

The maps that cover the entire SUW from west to east are given below for reference.

OS Landranger Series (1:50,000)
(9 sheets cover the whole of the SUW)

Sheet 82: Stranraer & Glenluce
Sheet 76: Girvan
Sheet 77: Dalmellington & New Galloway
Sheet 71: Lanark & Upper Nithsdale[*]
Sheet 78: Nithsdale & Annandale
Sheet 79: Hawick & Eskdale
Sheet 73: Peebles, Galashiels & Selkirk
Sheet 74: Kelso & Coldstream
Sheet 67: Duns, Dunbar & Eyemouth

[*] Sheet 71 is unnecessary if Sheet 77 and Sheet 78 are used, as there is sheet overlap.

The route of the SUW is clearly shown on these Landranger maps as a line of red diamond symbols.

OS Explorer Series (1:25,000)
(13 sheets cover the whole of the SUW)

Sheet 309: Stranraer & The Rhins
Sheet 310: Glenluce & Kirkcowan
Sheet 319: Galloway Forest Park South
Sheet 318: Galloway Forest Park North [*]

Sheet 320: Castle Douglas, Loch Ken & New Galloway
Sheet 328: Sanquhar & New Cumnock
Sheet 329: Lowther Hills, Sanquhar & Leadhills
Sheet 330: Moffat & St Mary's Loch
Sheet 322: Annandale, Annan, Lockerbie & Beattock
Sheet 337: Peebles & Innerleithen
Sheet 338: Galashiels, Selkirk & Melrose
Sheet 345: Lammermuir Hills
Sheet 346: Berwick-upon-Tweed, Eyemouth & Duns, St Abb's Head & Cockburnspath

[*] Sheet 318 is unnecessary if Sheet 319 and Sheet 320 are used, as there is sheet overlap.

The route of the SUW is clearly shown on these Explorer maps as a line of green diamond symbols.

Harvey's Maps
A few of the maps produced by Harvey Maps (12–22 Main Street, Doune, Perthshire FK16 6BJ; **www.harveymaps.co.uk**) are useful for SUW Walkers. The following sheets provide mapping of some of the areas through which the SUW passes:
Superwalker Map (1:25,000): Galloway Hills
Walker's Map (1:40,000): Lowther Hills
Walker's Map (1:40,000): Peebles (Manor Hills).

NAVIGATING ALONG THE SUW

The entire length of the Southern Upland Way is waymarked with a special white Scottish Thistle Symbol, identical to that used on all the other National Trails in Scotland (West Highland Way, Great Glen Way and Speyside Way). These waymarks appear most often on wooden posts, which usually also carry yellow directional arrows. Where the Way crosses public roads and at other important junctions along the route, SUW signposts have been erected. In general within Dumfries & Galloway these signposts are of wood, whereas in the Borders Region they tend to be of metal, and painted green.

Other Trail 'furniture' includes ladder stiles and stone stiles over dry stone walls (called dry stane dykes in Scotland), and wooden stiles over fences. These are quite numerous and are generally in good condition, as are the many wooden bridges and short sections of duck boarding (the latter over boggy areas) found along the Way. Never cross walls or fences except at the indicated points, where stiles or gates are always to be used. Some of the man-made wooden structures (ladder and other stiles and duck boarding) can be very slippery,

Footpath signposts at Lauder (Stage 12)

particularly when wet or icy. Many are protected by non-slippery surfaces, or wire netting, although in some cases these are too old and worn to be completely effective. The ground is sometimes rough and over-grown with long reed grasses and other vegetation, particularly during the summer months, so that care is required when placing feet in order to avoid ankle or knee sprains, or worse. So do take care: alertness, concentration and care are major factors for a safe journey along the SUW.

Following the Way in good conditions is generally quite straight-forward, but does require some skills in map reading and compass work, particularly on the upland sections of the Trail when hill fog covers the landscape. Inadvertently drifting from the line of the Way could lead to disastrous results in some of the large and featureless expanses of hill and moorland through which the SUW passes. Be vigilant in navigation at all times, particularly in inclement weather conditions. Only experi-enced hill walkers should contemplate leaving the Way to take in nearby hills or following their own alternative routes. Waymarking else-where in the Southern Uplands is largely non-existent, and there are few paths other than those formed by the use of quad bikes by shepherds in recent decades.

It is advisable to take along addi-tional maps to those of the Way provided in this guidebook (see 'Maps' above) and a compass should most definitely be carried, together with a knowledge of how to use it. On some sections across open moorland, waymarker posts are not always easily visible and paths are thin or non-exis-tent in places, so that in these areas a compass is an indispensable tool. A

A SUW marker post above Blackhouse (Stage 9)

GPS is not an essential item of equipment, but some may find it a comfort to carry one, and such a device would certainly be useful in mist, particularly if high level alternatives or day hill walks off the SUW are anticipated. A GPS would be useful if the route of the SUW is completely lost, in order to determine one's position, but never rely on one of these instruments entirely; a map and compass are the fundamentals.

There have been a fair number of route changes over the years from the original line of the SUW. On the whole these route realignments, which are generally well waymarked, represent a considerable improvement to the Way, and for this the SUW rangers are to be congratulated. Two of the best examples are the new route over Craigairie Fell (Stage 3) and the new hill section after Loch Trool (Stage 4).

ACCESS IN SCOTLAND

The Land Reform (Scotland) Act became law in 2005. This gives considerable statutory rights of access to the outdoors, one of the most enlightened acts of its type in all Europe. But never forget that these rights of access come with important responsibilities. It is a good idea, if unfamiliar with walking in Scotland, to acquaint yourself with the new access code by referring to the free leaflet entitled 'Scottish Outdoor Access Code – Know the Code before you go', available from Tourist Information Centres in Scotland or visit **www.outdooraccess-scotland.com**.

SUW INFORMATION LEAFLETS AND BOARDS

At various locations along the SUW within Dumfries & Galloway, between Portpatrick and Ettrick Head, the first 200km (125 miles) of the route, weather-protected boxes will be found containing (hopefully) a variety of free information leaflets. The boxes are normally kept topped up during the main walking season, from Easter to the autumn, by the local Ranger Service. Separate leaflet guides are available on such topics as Trees and Shrubs, Wildlife, Geology, Archaeology, Place Names and the Killing Times. The SUW Official Accommodation Guide is usually to be found amongst these leaflets. Unfortunately this is not a service operated by the Borders Ranger Service and consequently none will be found east of Ettrick Head. These free leaflets are also usually available from local tourist offices, including those in the Borders.

At regular intervals along the length of the SUW the Rangers have erected very informative boards detailing various aspects of the Way and the surrounding countryside. Each board has specific information on the area in which it is situated. The locations of the many SUW Information

Boards are given in the various 'Route' sections of the Trail Guide.

During 2005, as part of the celebrations of the 21st Anniversary of the SUW (opened in April 1984), thirteen artist-made boxes called 'kists' were hidden at locations along the SUW, one on each of the thirteen stages. Inside each box was a hoard of special 'waymerks', small lead or copper tokens marked with tiny, minted images. These represented some aspect of the archaeology, history or wildlife of the area of the hiding place. The Waymerks project proved popular with people walking the Way in search of these special mementoes.

THE E2

The SUW forms a significant part of the E2, which is one of several ultra-long-distance walking trails through Europe. The E2 is 2910 miles (4850km) in length and runs from Nice in southern France to Galway in Ireland. From Nice it travels north through the Alps, Jura, Vosges, Alsace-Lorraine, Luxembourg, Belgium and Holland. On the British side of the Channel there are two optional routes through England, one from Dover and one from Harwich. These join at Kirk Yetholm, the northern terminus of the Pennine Way. In Scotland the E2 follows St Cuthbert's Way to Melrose where it picks up the SUW Way, which it follows all the way west to Stranraer. A ferry then leads to Ireland for the

last stages of this mammoth walk, which ends at the Atlantic on the Galway coast. As a walk of a lifetime the E2 through Europe can be thoroughly recommended as it passes through a tremendous variety of landscapes and cultures, from the polders of Holland to the high Alps of France, from the fen country of East Anglia to the Southern Uplands of Scotland. Signs for the E2 will be seen in the Borders attached to SUW signposts.

TICKS

Tick populations appear to be on the increase in the upland areas of Britain. Although the author encountered none on his last coast to coast crossing, there have been warnings from some other SUW walkers. The usual hosts of the tick are sheep and deer, but care should be exercised to avoid getting bitten yourself, as ticks are carriers of Lyme's Disease, a serious condition. It should not be cause for great concern, nor spoil your walk, but do be aware of the problem; really only common sense is required.

Long trousers rather than shorts are advisable as ticks are most commonly picked up from vegetation along the route. Waterproof trousers or overtrousers are particularly recommended, as soaking wet and tall grasses and other dense vegetation will probably be frequently encountered. Even if it is not raining at the time overgrown vegetation can remain very wet for a long time after

Bust of Sir Walter Scott, Galashiels (Stage 10)

a downpour and the extra leg protection will also help to avoid ticks.

Check the skin frequently for ticks and if found remove them at once, taking care not to leave the mouthparts still attached (a special small tool can be purchased for this purpose).

COMPLETION CERTIFICATES AND SUW BADGES

Attractive high quality completion certificates are available free of charge to all those who have walked the entire route of the SUW, whether in a single crossing, or as a series of shorter walks. They make excellent mementoes of your achievement and are nice souvenirs of your walking holiday(s). They are available from the Countryside Ranger Services of either Dumfries & Galloway or the Scottish Borders (see Appendix 3). It is best to apply for a certificate by filling in one of the Certificate Application Forms that are usually present in the free Southern Upland Way

Accommodation Guides, available from local Tourist Information Centres or in the special SUW Leaflet Boxes places at various locations en route. Certificates for those who have walked only part of the way are also available.

Cloth SUW badges are also usually available, for a small price, at various local outlets.

their SUW trek and will want to return again and again, to explore the area more fully, walk more of the hill ranges and even attempt a bespoke coast to coast crossing of this wonderful region. Knowledge and experience of the area gained whilst on the SUW will well equip the walker for such future visits and ventures.

A HIGH LEVEL ALTERNATIVE COAST TO COAST ROUTE

Suitably experienced hill walkers and backpackers may wish to devise their own high level coast to coast route across the Southern Uplands. It is possible to plan and execute several such routes of varying levels of difficulty. From west to east the main ranges to consider crossing are the Galloway Hills, Carsphairn Hills, Lowther Hills, Moffat Hills, Manor or Tweedsmuir Hills, the Moorfoots and the Lammermuir Hills. Such an adventure would be a considerable undertaking, far in excess of that of walking the SUW. The Southern Upland Way provides access to most of these ranges and could form the principle means of linking up the high level sections. Information gleaned from this guidebook as well as in the SMC guide to the Southern Uplands (see Appendix 2) should prove helpful to those planning their own routes across these hills. It is hoped that those who have not previously walked in the Southern Uplands will develop a love of this area during

NOTES ON USING THIS GUIDEBOOK

The SUW has been divided into 13 stages in this guidebook. Each stage starts and finishes at a location where there is at least B&B accommodation, but often there are other options for an overnight stay, hotel, youth hostel or campsite. Most of these stages are intended to be walked in one day, but some of them are too long for many walkers. In particular Stages 4, 5, 7 and 8 are all over 20 miles in length. They appear as stages of this length because there is no possibility of shortening them by staying overnight at an intermediate location, apart from wild camping or overnighting in a bothy. However, commercial organisations operate vehicle pick-up services, details of which are given in the Trail Guide, that allow these stages to be shortened into more manageable day walks.

Each stage begins with a 'summary table' that shows at a glance the total distance for the stage and the distances between intermediate points, in both miles and

Highland cattle on the SUW east of Loch Trool (Stage 4)

kilometres. The 'Summary' which follows is intended to provide an overview of the stage and could usefully be read the evening before the section is undertaken to give a feel for the nature of the forthcoming walk. Any possible problems and alternatives are discussed here.

The detailed route description that follows is intended for use when walking the Way in conjunction with the appropriate map. Special attention has been given to areas where there are likely to be navigational problems. There are several new sections of the route that have replaced the original

33

line of the SUW. In these cases, which are all clearly identified in the relevant sections of the Trail Guide, particular care has been taken in describing the new route (note that some old maps may not show these new routes).

Distances are given in the 'Route' section of the Trail Guide only in metres and kilometres, as OS maps are metric and to quote imperial units as well would be tedious and would clutter the text with too many conversions. Any readers still unfamiliar with metric units of distance are reminded that a metre is just a little over a yard, and that to convert kilometres to miles divide by 1.6 (approximately). Summits and other heights are given in both metres and feet, as many British walkers find it easier to visualise height in feet rather than the metres now marked on OS maps.

Finally each stage closes with a 'Places of Interest' section that provides concise but adequate information on the many towns, villages, country houses, gardens, monuments, etc, on or close to the route. In a few instances the subjects described in this section are not actually 'places' but are other items of interest to the SUW walker (the 'Killing Times' described in Stage 3 is one example).

This information will enable the SUW walker to appreciate in full the areas through which he or she is passing, and allow decisions to be made as to which places to spend further time exploring. Part of the joy of walking a long distant route through an area new to the walker is having the chance to explore previously undiscovered places and learn about the history and topography of the area. All SUW trekkers should take some time out from their walk to visit one or more of the many places of interest on the route. The main places of particular merit to visit en route, where no or very little detour from the line of the Way is necessary, are in summary:

• Castle Kennedy Gardens (Stages 1/2)
• Lead Mining Museum, Wanlockhead (Stage 6)
• Traquair House (Stage 9)
• Melrose Abbey (Stages 10/11)
• Thirlestane Castle and Gardens, Lauder (Stages 11/12)

The walking stages associated with most of these attractions are relatively short, such that time should be available to allow an extended visit.

STAGE 1

Portpatrick to Castle Kennedy

13.4 miles (21.6km)

	Distance (miles)		Distance (km)	
	Sectional	Cumulative	Sectional	Cumulative
Portpatrick	0	0	0	0
Killantringan Lighthouse				
(Black Head)	2.4	2.4	3.9	3.9
B738	1.2	3.6	1.9	5.8
Piltanton Burn				
(Greenfield Farm)	3.9	7.5	6.3	12.1
A77 (Whiteleys Farm)	2.5	10.0	4.0	16.1
Railway line	2.6	12.6	4.2	20.3
Castle Kennedy (A75)	0.8	13.4	1.3	21.6

Summary

The walk starts with a highly scenic section of about 3.5km of coastal walking, along cliff tops and down to small coves and beaches. Some care is required on the cliff sections on the first half of this route from Portpatrick. At the Killantringan Lighthouse on Black Point the trail leaves the coast to head eastwards on minor lanes and tracks across the Rhins peninsula, reaching its high point on this stage at 156m (512ft) on Broad Moor. Knockquhassen Reservoir is passed on a good path to its south, after which the Way descends towards Stranraer and Loch Ryan. The SUW does not enter Stranraer itself, although a diversion of less than a mile would allow a visit to this town, the capital of the Rhins and a major port to Larne near Belfast in Northern Ireland. The route skirts to the south of Stranraer, but offers good views down to the town and Loch Ryan, as it makes its way via narrow lanes, tracks and paths to

Castle Kennedy, a small village on the A75, and home to the renowned and eponymous gardens.

This first stage of the SUW is a short one for a

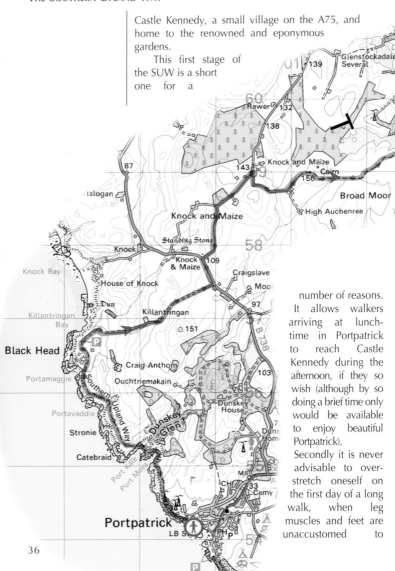

number of reasons. It allows walkers arriving at lunch-time in Portpatrick to reach Castle Kennedy during the afternoon, if they so wish (although by so doing a brief time only would be available to enjoy beautiful Portpatrick).

Secondly it is never advisable to over-stretch oneself on the first day of a long walk, when leg muscles and feet are unaccustomed to

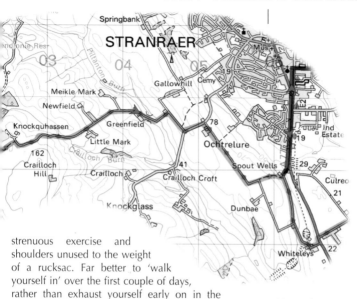

Map continues p. 38

strenuous exercise and shoulders unused to the weight of a rucksac. Far better to 'walk yourself in' over the first couple of days, rather than exhaust yourself early on in the adventure. There is plenty of opportunity to do just that in the days to come! Tomorrow is also a short day, designed to allow sufficient time to visit the Castle Kennedy Gardens. These two moderate days will hopefully have increased your fitness and you will by then be prepared for the more rigorous days to come. Strong, fit and experienced walkers could nevertheless reach New Luce on the first day if they so desired.

Route

To commence the SUW, head for the north-west end of **Portpatrick** harbour (toilets) to reach a SUW Information Board, the first of many encountered along the Way, and the very first SUW wooden fingerpost, situated at the foot of a long flight of concrete steps, heading up the coastal cliff. These mark the start of your 212-mile (341km) epic journey eastwards to Cockburnspath. But for the first few miles you stay with the west coast, enjoying an excellent

37

SUW Board –
Portpatrick

*Special care is
required on this first
section of the SUW,
along this rocky
coastline, particu-
larly in wet, windy
or icy conditions.*

coastal path. Note the various dates from historic, prehistoric and geological times marked on these steps. Head
up to the huge Portpatrick Hotel with its Scottish
Baronial architecture.

Take the good path at the top of the steps,
heading northwards and finally pulling away from
Portpatrick. There are benches here if you wish to
linger awhile to admire the view. ◄ The path at
this point is protected from the steep drop down
to the cliffs below by a sturdy wooden fence.
Walk to the left of the British Telecom Radio
Station, still on the good coastal path above the
cliffs. When Portpatrick Golf Course comes into
view go up a short flight of wooden steps to turn
left along an asphalted drive alongside this golf
course, but soon leaving this hard surface for the
continuing coastal path. The route descends over
rocks to reach a sandy and shingle beach. Cross
this to climb back onto the peninsula headland,
soon dropping again to cross a wooden footbridge.
Follow the thistle waymarks carefully to the right of a

huge boulder rock face, and so up a steep rocky, chain-assisted climb, back onto the grassy coastal path, which is met at a stile. An excellent section follows where it is possible to stride out on green springy turf. Soon the lighthouse (Killantringan Lighthouse – private) at **Black Head** will come into view. Continue ahead until you almost reach the lighthouse, to a SUW fingerpost that will direct you to the right and inland. At last you are on your long journey to the east coast! ▶

A narrow asphalted lane climbs gradually eastwards away from the coast passing first Killantringan Farmhouse and then Killantringan Cottage, after which it levels and continues to a main road, the B738. Go left on this usually fairly quiet road for about 400m to turn right onto a narrow lane that rises gently over a rounded green hill. Remain on this lane as it bends first to the left and then to the right to pass to the left of a farm. About 350m later turn sharp right off this lane at a SUW fingerpost onto a gravel track by a solitary house. Follow this track up onto **Broad Moor**, passing to the left of another solitary

Before you turn inland be sure to enjoy the grand view of Knock Bay and the coastal cliffs to the north.

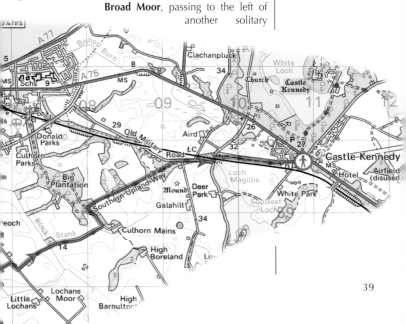

39

Looking back to Portpatrick

From this point, Mulloch Hill at 156m (512ft) on Broad Moor, the tiny steep-sided volcanic island of Ailsa Craig in the Firth of Clyde to the north can just be seen on a very clear day.

house and garage, after which the track becomes grassy (a box with free SUW leaflets will hopefully be passed on your left). Pass over a stile to enter pasture and climb to a SUW marker post at the top of a grassy hill, and bear left here as indicated. ◄

Cross another stile and follow a path eastward, now with a loch (Knockquhassen Reservoir) clearly visible over to your left. This pleasant path passes this loch, eventually emerging at a track. Turn right onto this track, which eventually becomes a narrow metalled lane. Follow this gently downhill to cross **Piltanton Burn** at Greenfield Farm. The lane then bears left and climbs, later veering right to reach the main road between Stranraer and Portpatrick. Turn left along this road for about 250m where, at Cottfield House turn right onto a lane (there is a good view down to Stranraer and its sea loch, Loch Ryan, from here). The narrow lane runs dead straight for a kilometre before turning left. After about 100m, where the road bends sharply to the right, walk

40

ahead on a grassy path between hedge and fence. This descends to a minor road where turn right (SUW finger-post) uphill. Ignore a right turn (no waymark here in July 2005), but continue now downhill, past the house of Stanalane. On reaching the busy A77 road at Whiteleys Farm, cross it with care and turn left along the footpath following this road, but only for about 50m. Turn right onto a track alongside trees. Follow this to another lane where turn right for about 150m and then left onto another minor lane which descends and continues to reach a road at a T-junction. Turn left onto a track here, with a wood now on your right.

After about 250m turn right onto another track through the wood, then out into an open area before re-entering woodland. Continue on this pleasant track until it reaches a minor road at a T-junction. Turn right along this narrow lane for about 350m to another T-junction. Turn left here to pass under a railway line and then follow the lane for about 50m to turn off it onto a path

Coast north of Portpatrick

41

through woodland. This follows the course of the railway line, which is a little over to the right. Eventually the buildings of **Castle Kennedy** will become visible through the trees over to the left. A SUW Information Board is met at the edge of a housing estate. Continue ahead (east) passing Castle Kennedy School on your left, soon bearing left to reach the very busy A75 trunk road, opposite the entrance to Castle Kennedy Gardens. For the SUW continue ahead on the drive of the Gardens, or if staying the night in the Plantings Hotel, Castle Kennedy, turn right to follow the pavement for about 400m to reach the hotel, which is on your right (note that there is a small store in the petrol garage on the A75).

PLACES OF INTEREST

Portpatrick

No more splendid starting place for the SUW can be imagined than pretty little Portpatrick on the rocky west coast of the Rhins peninsula. Portpatrick is a lovely small coastal town with its blue, white and cream brightly painted buildings huddled around an attractive horse-shoe shaped bay and neat harbour. There is plenty of accommodation on offer in the town, from harbourside hotel to B&B, but note that booking is well advised, particularly during the main summer season, as Portpatrick is a popular place for a holiday or short break and it would be a very pleasant place to spend the evening before venturing out on your long walk. One could be forgiven for thinking that you were in the Scottish Highlands or Islands from the surrounding landscape. Indeed the BBC in the early 2000's conned its viewers into believing that this area was one of the Hebridean Islands in a popular TV series, *Two Thousand Acres of Sky* (photographs of the cast of this series can be viewed by clients of one of the harbourside café/restaurants). Portpatrick and its harbour also wouldn't be out-of-place on the Cornish Coast. If you are arriving here on the midday bus from Stranraer then there are several cafes and restaurants awaiting you, for lunch or tea and coffee before setting out on the Way.

Although today the town is mainly of interest to tourists and television directors, in former times it was a major port to Ireland. Indeed the very name of the town, after the Irish patron saint, indicates its importance with communications and trade with Ireland. In its heyday in 1812, 20,000 horses and cattle were imported here from the Irish port of Donaghadee, a mere 21 miles away across the North Channel. Troops were sent to Ireland from Britain via Portpatrick, the town having a large and permanent barracks, and many Covenanters sailed from here to safety in Ireland. It was also the Gretna Green for Ireland, offering a quick and easy marriage with few questions asked. Even Peter the Great is said to have spent a night here on his visit to Britain in 1698. But by the 1840s, after the invention of the large and faster steamship that soon superseded sail, Portpatrick had fallen rapidly into decline as Stranraer was developed.

Killantringan Lighthouse
This lighthouse, which was built in 1900, marks the point where the SUW, having first followed the coast northwards from Portpatrick for about 3.5km, finally leaves the

Knock Bay from Killantringan Lighthouse

43

Note that the lighthouse is private property and the occupants should not be disturbed.

sea to commence its long journey to the east coast. The lighthouse apparently did not do its duty too well, as in 1982 a cargo ship ran aground on the nearby rocks spilling toxic waste into the sea and polluting the nearby coast. ◄

The Rhins

The first stage of the SUW involves a crossing of the Rhins peninsula, properly known as the Rhins of Galloway. It has a very distinctive shape, an elongated hammerhead, a long and fairly narrow wedge of pastoral green countryside, which is only prevented from being an island by the low-lying isthmus between Loch Ryan to the north and Luce Bay to the south. The word 'Rhins' comes from the Old Irish word 'Rind' meaning a headland.

Stranraer

The largest town in Galloway and the main port from Scotland to Northern Ireland, with regular sailings to Larne near Belfast. In the 17th century Stranraer (pronounced 'Stran-raa') had only a few hundred inhabitants, but the population later increased dramatically with the introduction of larger seafaring craft which found the deep waters of Loch Ryan more suitable for anchorage than the shallow harbour of Portpatrick. The SUW does not enter the town itself, but there are good views down to it and Loch Ryan as the Way skirts to the south. There is plentiful accommodation and many shops in the town which can be reached by a short detour off-route or by bus along the A75 from Castle Kennedy. Notable buildings include the 16th-century castle, used as a prison house during the Killing Times (see under 'Places of Interest' in Stage 3) and the North-West Castle, home of the famous Arctic explorer Sir John Ross in the early 19th century. Stranraer Museum (open daily except Sunday, all year, free admission), which details the history of Wigtownshire, is housed in the Old Town Hall that dates from 1776. The Tourist Office has an excellent 'town trail' leaflet which will allow you to learn much more about the town as you wander its streets.

STAGE 2

Castle Kennedy to New Luce

8.9 miles (14.3km) + 1 mile (1.6km)

	Distance (miles)		Distance (km)	
	Sectional	Cumulative	Sectional	Cumulative
Castle Kennedy (A 75)	0	13.4	0	21.6
Castle Kennedy Gardens	0.6	14.0	1.0	22.6
Water of Luce Footbridge	5.1	19.1	8.2	30.8
GR NX192650				
(minor road ENE of				
New Luce)	3.2	22.3*	5.1	35.9*
New Luce	(1.0)	22.3*	(1.6)	35.9*

* New Luce is a 1 mile (1.6km) detour from the SUW. This distance is not added to the
   cumulative distance along the SUW.

Summary
The highlight of the Way in this area is the Castle
Kennedy Gardens, and time should most certainly be
allocated for a visit. If the morning is dedicated to the
Gardens (and an early start is not required as the Gardens
do not open until 10am) then the section of the SUW can
comfortably be accomplished in an afternoon, particularly if one opts for the shorter direct route into New Luce
from the Glenluce to New Luce Road.

After the Gardens, the Way heads eastwards offering
a final glimpse of Loch Ryan and the west coast. Take a
long last look at Loch Ryan, for you will not see the sea
again until the Scottish east coast is reached a little before
Cockburnspath. The trail follows a path around a now
harvested conifer plantation, and crosses the main
railway line between Stranraer and Glasgow before
heading off across a section of the desolate moorland of
Kilhern Moss, an area rich in archaeological history.

Finally the SUW is temporarily left behind for a gentle descent to the charming village of New Luce. Sleep well tonight, for tomorrow the walk will continue in earnest.

Route

From the gatehouse of **Castle Kennedy Gardens** turn north off the A75 to walk along the drive following the sign for the Gardens. The first of the two lochs that surround the Gardens, White Loch, soon comes into view. Follow the long drive, which is ablaze with rhododendron and azalea flowers during springtime, passing to the right of the loch. After a little over a kilometre you will reach a drive junction at the 'bus park' for the Gardens. The SUW heads off to the right here, but for a visit to Castle Kennedy Gardens turn left through the wrought iron gates.

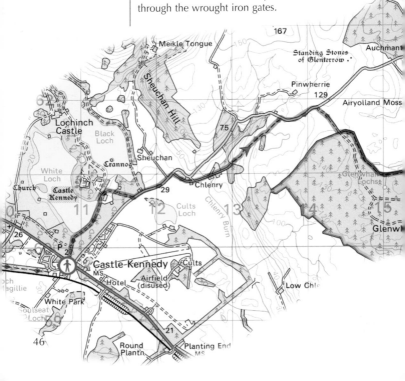

After your visit to the Gardens, a 'must', return to the 'bus park' to follow the SUW sign heading eastwards. The track leads to the Castle Douglas to New Luce Road, where you turn left for about 800m. A delightful rural scene soon opens out, of rich fields and gentle wooded hills, with Cults Loch over to your right.

This board indicates the alternative route to New Luce and out again along the road to rejoin, east of New Luce, the standard route that bypasses the village, an option you might want to consider if the day is late.

About 50m before this road bends to the right, turn right onto a track at a SUW fingerpost. The route passes the houses of Balnab and **Chlenry**, after which it begins a climb that amounts to around 100m (328ft) of ascent in total. After crossing a stile the route climbs steeply to reach open country. Head north-eastwards, keeping scrub, low wall and fence on your left. Climb two ladder stiles to reach a grassy track junction: take the left fork that leads back to the Castle Kennedy to New Luce Road. Follow the road ahead for about 500m to reach a SUW Information Board and fingerpost. ◄

Turn right at the Information Board along a gravel track heading south-east. At a gate and stile turn left on a footpath (note that this is the start of a new route, differing from the original line of the SUW between here and the railway line). The path is generally well defined, although in places overgrown with rosebay willowherb, reedy grasses and thistles during the summer months, and passes to the left of an area from which a tree plantation has been harvested. The path follows a dry stone wall (dyke) on the left for most of its length. In the 1980s and 1990s there was considerably more forestry in this area than nowadays, but the harvesting has produced a fairly unattractive section of the Way. Note the tall turbines of a wind farm to the north-east, which will be approached on tomorrow's walk from New Luce.

The path eventually reaches the edge of mixed woodland where it bears left to enter the trees. Proceed until you meet a waymarker post that blocks the path: turn left here, downhill through the trees to cross Craig Burn by a wooden footbridge. Continue uphill on a thin path, with the railway line over to your right, to cross a stile. You may have to negotiate head high bracken and other unfriendly vegetation in the summer months on the next section, before two stiles lead to a bridge over the railway line. A path descends through more bracken and then grass to reach, follow and eventually cross the **Water of Luce** by a most impressive suspension bridge. Cross a grassy field and then climb a steep bank to reach the Glenluce to New Luce road. Turn left.

New Luce

After about 200m, opposite the entrance to a farm, those staying overnight in New Luce have a choice of routes. The shortest way to **New Luce** is to remain on the road, along which the village is reached within a couple of kilometres. But the official route of the SUW turns right here to pass to the south of New Luce. It will later emerge on a minor lane about 1.6km to the east of New Luce. Those not staying overnight in New Luce and not wishing to visit the village should definitely take the official SUW trail across Kilhern Moss, which is a much better route than that along the road, although the latter is rarely very busy.

To continue along the SUW turn right off the road onto a track at the SUW fingerpost opposite the farm. Climb on this to reach a stile and open country. Continue on a grassy track with a dry stone wall (dyke) on your left. Cross another stile and continue on the dead straight grassy track across moorland, the wind farm visible ahead left. Another stile is crossed after which the track curves leftwards to aim straight towards the wind farm. The track climbs gradually to the ruins of the buildings of Kilhern. Just before reaching them turn left at a waymarker post, now heading north-west. Soon climb over another stile and turn left at another SUW marker post. The buildings of New Luce and Barnshangan farm soon come into view ahead.

Continue on this track until a gate is reached in a dry stone wall (dyke). Here leave the track as indicated by a marker post to pass to the left of a small plantation (note that the original line of the SUW went to the right of this plantation on the track). The path rejoins the track on the far side of the plantation: turn left along it to reach after about 250m a metalled track at a SUW Information Board and fingerpost. Those staying overnight in New Luce and who didn't take the shorter option to New Luce earlier, should turn left here for an easy walk of just over 1.5km. The official route of the SUW turns to the right, east-north-east, and those overnighting in New Luce should first return to this point the next morning.

New Luce nestles in a lush sylvan setting, a charming rural scene opening out as one gently descends the lane towards the small village. This detour from the SUW to New Luce takes about 20 minutes of easy walking.

PLACES OF INTEREST

Castle Kennedy

The Kennedys were the most powerful family in the area from the middle of the 15th century until the time of the Covenanters in the 1680s. The present settlement is named after the family seat, the castle having being built by the Kennedys in around 1607. The estates were later acquired by the Dalrymples of Stair. Only the ruins of the castle remain today, following a disastrous accidental fire in 1716.

Castle Kennedy House and Gardens

Castle Kennedy Gardens

These magnificent gardens are a highlight of the western stage of the walk, and walkers are strongly advised to pay a visit. No detour is necessary as the SUW passes the main entrance. The gardens, the oldest in south-west Scotland, occupy a 75 acre site between two large natural lochs, the White Loch and the Black Loch, and were laid out originally in the 18th century by the Second Earl of Stair, a former Ambassador to France and a general in the Wars of the Succession. Originally constructed and maintained by an army of men and horses, the gardens are nowadays tended by only three full-time gardeners! The gardens are particularly famous for their displays of rhododendrons and azaleas, and for the long avenue of enormous monkey-puzzle trees. Castle Kennedy Gardens, managed by the Stair Estate, are open from 1st April (or from Easter if earlier) to the end of September, seven days a week, from 10.00am to 5pm. There is a moderate entrance fee. Allow a minimum of two hours to do the gardens justice and expect to walk at least 2–4 km around this huge garden. During your visit be sure not to miss the:

- walled garden – this is at its best during July and early August
- sunken garden near Lochinch Castle
- wonderful display of rhododendrons and azaleas if visiting in springtime
- Monkey Puzzle Tree Avenue.

There is a teashop (tea, coffee and cakes sold here) at the entrance to the Garden, with toilets situated nearby.

Belties

Hopefully sometime during your walk across the Southern Uplands you will spot in the fields some of the distinctive belted Galloway cattle known locally and affectionately as 'Belties'. They can hardly be mistaken as they are jet-black coated beasts (less commonly brown coated) with a wide white band around the centre of the body. They are hardy animals, a necessary qualification in this part of the country, and above all else are *the* symbol of the region. The breed teetered close to extinction during the terrible scourge of foot and mouth disease that devastated Dumfries & Galloway in 2001, but they have now recovered well and are once more thriving in the rolling grassy hills and fields of southern Scotland.

New Luce

The village and its environs are known by some as 'Little England' a reference to the considerable numbers of English who have purportedly settled here. The main place of interest is the Church, which has some interesting old tombstones in its graveyard and is associated with the Covenanters (see the 'Killing Times' under 'Places of Interest' in Stage 3). The minister of New Luce Kirk from 1659 to 1662 was one Alexander Peden, a notable Covenanter. He fled his ministry on persecution to preach in the Galloway Hills and was for a time imprisoned on the Bass Rock (you will see this huge island rock in the Firth of Forth on your last day on the SUW – see Stage 13). Dubbed as Peden the Prophet he was said to be able to foretell the future. He died in 1686. Facilities in the village consist of a pub that offers bed and breakfast, another B&B establishment, and a small shop that sells snacks and drinks.

STAGE 3

New Luce to Bargrennan

17.8 miles (28.6km) + 1 mile (1.6km)

	Distance (miles)		Distance (km)	
	Sectional	Cumulative	Sectional	Cumulative
New Luce	0	22.3*	0	35.9*
GR NX192650 (minor road ENE of New Luce)	(1.0)	22.3*	(1.6)	35.9*
Laggangarn Standing Stones	5.1	27.4	8.2	44.1
Craig Airie Fell (320m)	1.5	28.9	2.4	46.5
Loch Derry	1.8	30.7	2.9	49.4
Darloskine Bridge	2.3	33.0	3.6	53.0
Knowe	2.7	35.7	4.4	57.4
Ochiltree Hill (184m)	2.1	37.8	3.5	60.9
Bargrennan	2.3	40.1	3.6	64.5

* New Luce is a 1 mile (1.6km) detour from the SUW. This distance is not added to the cumulative distance along the SUW.

Summary

There are many sights of interest on today's route. Soon after saying your goodbyes to the village of New Luce be sure not to miss the small hidden waterfall on the river known as the Cross Water of Luce. An open moorland section then needs to be tackled, gradually climbing north-eastwards into the hills. The wind farm that was seen from a distance yesterday is unfortunately to be encountered at fairly close quarters today. It was erected in 2004. A mixture of open hillside and forestry takes the walker past the novel beehive bothy and the prehistoric standing stones of Laggangarn. After passing a turn-off for the Wells of the Rees, the Way leads up to the summit of Craig Airie, at 320m (1050ft) the first time that the west-to-east SUW walker has been above the 1000ft contour

Waterfall on the Water of Luce

line. The view of the distant Galloway Hills and of the sea and Mull of Galloway from this summit is extensive. Much easier track walking is then on offer, taking the walker south-east to the first main road, the B7027, since leaving New Luce, now about 23km (over 14 miles) behind you.

A short, but tough section through steep woodland follows, but this is soon forgotten on the first-rate walk over Ochiltree Hill from whose 184m (604ft) summit there are now close-up views of the Galloway Hills, that the Way and you will soon be entering. More cross-country walking after the summit leads the walker to Bargrennan and accommodation for the night, the end of your first long section of walking along the SUW. But the longest and hardest sections (Stages 4 and 5) are now imminent. Eat and rest well tonight in preparation for the long stage tomorrow over the hills to Dalry.

Route

It is important to note that once you have left the village of **New Luce** behind, then the next public road encountered on the SUW is around 23km (over 14 miles), the B7027 at the hamlet of Knowe. The next place where accommodation, food and drink are available is at Bargrennan, almost 29km (18 miles) away. Serving this remote section is a bothy, the Beehive, 8km (5 miles) after New Luce.

Return to the SUW Information Board and fingerpost, at the point where you left the SUW yesterday. Continue east-north-east along the narrow metalled lane. Soon you will be accompanied by the sound of rushing water.

Map continues p. 58

Blood Moss

211

Mullwharchar

Loch of Purgatory

68

Hut Circles

Cairn na Gath Long Cairn

Balmurrie Fell

adzean

67

143

Water of Luce

Mines (dis)

Balmurrie

66

Knockiebae

Barnshangan

Cairns

63

Cemy

P

PH

79

Waterfall

Burnt Mound

Farmstead

Dranigower

65

122

Kilhern Loch

Hardcroft

53 New Luce

Cairn

Caves of Kilhern Chambered Cairn

This is from a small waterfall on the nearby Cross Water of Luce, over to your left, but which is difficult to see from the lane. So search out a stone stile in the dry stone wall (dyke) on the left. Once over this a narrow path leads to an old bridge over the river, from where there is a good view of the waterfall. ▶

Return to the lane to continue along the SUW. Soon after the waterfall the River Luce and the SUW part company, as the river heads north-west and a trail is followed north-eastwards. Where the lane swings sharply to the right, leave it to walk ahead over a bridge, following a surfaced track (sign for a 'no through road') to **Balmurrie**. This well-surfaced drive climbs gradually to pass first Balmurrie Cottage and then Balmurrie Farm, both on your right. The farm has a large, attractive landscaped garden. Continue ahead, now on an unsurfaced gravel path. After about 400m, a little before a stone barn, the SUW takes a track on the left (a deviation from the original line of the SUW). Leave this track 5m after crossing a cattle grid/gate by turning right onto a grassy path climbing the hillside.

Do take great care at the bridge, as it may be unsafe.

Beehive Bothy

57

The path soon disappears amongst the grasses and care is required to follow the thistle waymarks displayed on short posts (on the author's visit the waymarking was poor in this area). Cross a fence by a stile and then a small footbridge over a tiny stream, keeping a north-north-east bearing with a dry stone wall (dyke) over to your right. The path and the waymarking improve as the original line of the SUW is resumed, but the pylons of the wind farm on the rocky hills to the right are something of a blot on this fine upper moorland landscape. Walkers who made this journey before 2004 were fortunate indeed not to have their view spoiled by these monsters.

The trail reaches a plantation. Here do not follow the clear grassy track along the edge of the plantation, but look for a stile over a fence into the plantation to pick up a path that follows a clear firebreak in the trees (again the

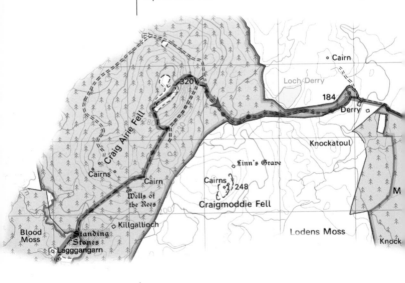

waymarking was poor in this area at the time of the author's visit). Follow this path through the firebreak until a forest track is reached, upon which you turn right. Some welcome easier walking leads in about 800m to a SUW fingerpost directing the walker onto a surfaced path through the trees to the right. This good path eventually leads to a clearing in the woods in which is situated the Beehive Bothy, the first of the six bothies on the Southern Upland Way (see Appendix 1). ▶

In the shape of a huge beehive, this wooden building offers good shelter, with wooden platforms for sitting and sleeping.

From the Beehive follow the path through grass (and high bracken during the summer) to reach two large standing stones, the **Laggangarn Standing Stones**, which date from 2000BC. Then cross a long wooden bridge over a stream to re-enter the conifer plantation. A short, rather claustrophobic section follows in which a good path is enclosed by dense trees. This emerges into a clearing and leads to a wide forest track. Cross over this track, following SUW waymarks, which head uphill. Climb on this path to reach a fingerpost, which indicates that it is a mile back to Laggangarn Standing Stones, and 100 yards off to the right to the Wells of the Rees.

Map continues p. 60

After a visit to the Wells of the Rees return to the main path to follow SUW waymarks carefully, often through areas of harvested woodland.

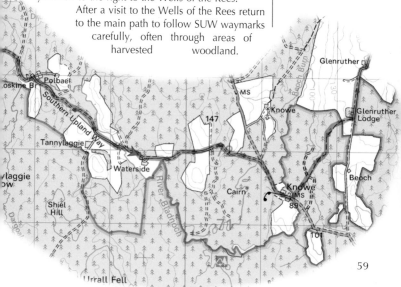

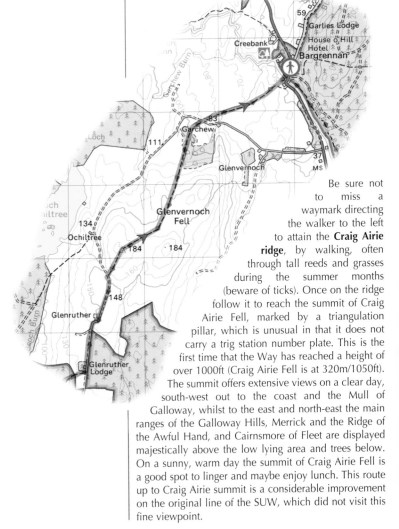

Be sure not to miss a waymark directing the walker to the left to attain the **Craig Airie ridge**, by walking, often through tall reeds and grasses during the summer months (beware of ticks). Once on the ridge follow it to reach the summit of Craig Airie Fell, marked by a triangulation pillar, which is unusual in that it does not carry a trig station number plate. This is the first time that the Way has reached a height of over 1000ft (Craig Airie Fell is at 320m/1050ft). The summit offers extensive views on a clear day, south-west out to the coast and the Mull of Galloway, whilst to the east and north-east the main ranges of the Galloway Hills, Merrick and the Ridge of the Awful Hand, and Cairnsmore of Fleet are displayed majestically above the low lying area and trees below. On a sunny, warm day the summit of Craig Airie Fell is a good spot to linger and maybe enjoy lunch. This route up to Craig Airie summit is a considerable improvement on the original line of the SUW, which did not visit this fine viewpoint.

Descend the hill on the ridge ahead following a good path to reach and cross a gravel track, heading towards Loch Derry. On meeting this gravel track a second time turn right along it. Remain on the track to pass a signpost indicating a detour to Linn's Tomb off to the right.

This wide gravel track offers easy walking, with the enticing Galloway Hills appearing ever closer. The track passes to the right (i.e. south) of **Loch Derry** and continues ahead. Eventually the roofs of Derry Farm come into view below right. The track heads north for a while (note the interesting pointed cairn on the hill ahead, shaped rather like an elongated dunce's hat) before swinging sharp right to descend towards Derry. ▶

Follow SUW waymarks at track junctions to head generally eastwards to reach a SUW fingerpost at **Darloskine Bridge**. Turn right here to cross the bridge and continue on a track now heading south-east. Eventually cross a bridge over the river Bladnoch and, after the house of Waterside, follow the surfaced lane until it reaches the B7027 road, the first major public road encountered since leaving New Luce.

Turn right to follow this road for about 800m to reach the hamlet of **Knowe**. The only facility here is a telephone box. At the far end of Knowe, immediately after a road bridge, turn left at a SUW fingerpost onto a footpath climbing up into the trees. Cross a forest track and continue north-east uphill through the plantation. Some care in navigation is required to follow the path that meanders through the forest, and the conditions underfoot in wet weather are sure to be boggy and unpleasant. However, less than a mile after leaving Knowe a poorly surfaced lane is encountered near to a bungalow (Glenruther Lodge). Turn left along this lane.

Pass to the right of **Glenruther** Farm, admiring the fine views of the Galloway Hills, now close at hand ahead and to the right. Directly ahead lies Ochiltree Hill, our next destination. On reaching a cattle grid and dry stone wall (dyke) bear right off this minor road onto a path that skirts the hillside and offers a fine view of **Loch Ochiltree** over to the left (north-west). The trail climbs to

There should be special boxes here that should contain SUW information leaflets.

the triangulation pillar on the 184m (604ft) summit of the hill (OS number plate S8223). It is a superb viewpoint, presenting a close panorama of the Galloway Hills that you will be traversing tomorrow. ◀

Head off north-eastwards from the summit on a thin path, slowly descending the hillside. The trail eventually reaches a road at a metal fieldgate and side gate. Turn right on this minor road. Just before reaching a farm, bear left off this lane as indicated by a SUW waymark. Walk over rough pasture to cross two ladder stiles and one stone stile to reach the A714 at **Bargrennan**. A Southern Upland Way Information board is situated here. Turn left along this road to walk over the road bridge. At the far side of this bridge, at a SUW fingerpost, turn right along the bank of the River Cree to continue the Way. But most walkers will be seeking accommodation for the night at Bargrennan. For the House o' Hill Hotel and the campsite (Glentrool Holiday Park) continue on the A714 for about 350m to take the Glen Trool Village road off on the right. The House o'Hill Hotel is 250m up here on the left and the campsite a little further.

This trig pillar has quite obviously been adopted by some individual or more likely group of people for whom it holds great affection, for at the time of the author's visit the pillar and its surrounding stones had been beautifully painted white.

Summit of Ochiltree Hill

PLACES OF INTEREST

The Killing Times

This wretched period of Scottish history began in 1638 at the National Covenant, where the Scottish Presbyterians, who objected to Episcopalian interference in their worship, pledged opposition to the English Bishops. But trouble was low key until the restoration of the monarchy in 1660, when Charles II took the English crown. The Covenanters, as they became known, were mercilessly persecuted and a great number were summarily executed, often in the open air when they were caught at illegal worship. One of the principal persecutors was John Graham of Claverhouse, known as 'Bloody Clavers'. The Pentland Rising, which began in St John Town of Dalry in 1666, was severely put down at a battle in the Pentland Hills near Edinburgh, and the Covenanters were also defeated at battles at Bothwell Bridge (1670) and at Airds Moss near Cumnock (1680). Persecution of the Covenanters was relaxed with the coming of William and Mary to the English throne in 1688 and the Killing Times were then thankfully largely over. The many monuments to the martyred Covenanters in southern Scotland are a vivid reminder of those troubled times. Several of these memorials are situated on or near to the SUW (see for example Linn's Grave, Allan's Cairn and Caldons).

Glenluce Abbey

A few miles south of New Luce lie the picturesque ruins of Glenluce Abbey alongside the Water of Luce. The Abbey Church, founded in 1190 by Roland, Lord of Galloway and occupied by Cistercian monks from Melrose, is today cared for by the National Trust for Scotland. There is a nominal entrance fee to this property, which is well worth a visit if transport can be arranged (open all year, restricted times October to Easter).

The Whithorn Pilgrim Way

Another long-distance trail leaves the SUW at New Luce to travel southwards for about 43 miles through the Machars of Galloway, a lush green, rolling rural area which contains the highest concentration of ancient monuments and ecclesiastical sites in Scotland. The trail follows a route similar to that taken by medieval pilgrims travelling from Stranraer and Ireland to Whithorn, a place of pilgrimage. It was here in about AD450, a century before St Columbus, that Christianity was first brought to British shores by Saint Ninian. Whithorn is one of the major centres of early Christianity in Europe, ranking alongside Iona and Lindisfarne on Holy Island in Britain and Santiago in northern Spain.

The route offers easy walking, mainly along pleasant minor country lanes and tracks, first to the picturesque ruins of the Cistercian Glenluce Abbey (see above) and then via Mochrum to the small town of Whithorn. The first-rate 'Whithorn Story' Visitor Centre and Museum, together with the ruins of the medieval priory, make for an interesting day in the town. The Pilgrim's Trail continues as a circular walk around the tip of the Machars Peninsula, visiting St Ninian's Cave on the rugged coast and St Ninian's Chapel at the port of the Isle of Whithorn, before returning to Whithorn town.

A walk along the SUW from Portpatrick to New Luce and then along the Pilgrim Way to the Isle of Whithorn would make a very pleasant walking holiday of about a week's duration, full of scenic, botanical and historical interest. The Machars peninsula is also the home of Scotland's Book Town, Wigtown, which vies with Hay-on-Wye as Britain's premier literary venue. The area around Monreith and Port William was the childhood home of Gavin Maxwell whose charming and sensitive book, *Ring of Bright Water*, tells the tale of his life with a tame otter, Midge. Otters still thankfully swim the rivers in this part of southern Scotland. The Otter Memorial to Gavin Maxwell overlooks Kirkmaiden Church at Monreith.

The route of the Pilgrim's Way is waymarked with blue 'Whithorn Pilgrim Way' signs at road junctions, and with a Celtic Cross symbol on the off-road sections. Much of it would also make a good route for cyclists. Unfortunately the original guidebook to the Pilgrim's Way (*A Way to Whithorn* by David Patterson – see Appendix 2) is now out of print, but can no doubt be acquired from specialist second-hand bookshops or perhaps from the Web. Even without the guidebook a route can easily be traced south down the Machars Peninsula.

Laggangarn Standing Stones

Laggangarn or Laggangairn Standing Stones are two ancient marker stones, dating from about 4000 years ago. Christian cross markings, clearly visible on the stones today, were made, it is thought, in about the 8th century. The stones were first studied by General Pitt-Rivers, the first Inspector of Ancient Monuments in Britain, who made drawings of the stones and their markings.

Laggangarn Standing Stones

Wells of the Rees

These three wells (of the Rees or Sheepfolds) are ancient structures whose origin is lost in antiquity. They are dome-like dry stone structures about a metre high and built over tiny springs. About 500m to the south-west is the site of the ancient church of Killgallioch.

Linn's Grave

About 500m off-route, on the slopes of Craigmoddie Fell, will be found the walled-in grave of one Alexander Linn, a shepherd and Covenanter from New Luce who was shot on this spot for his beliefs in 1685 by the King's dragoons under the command of Lieutenant-General Drumand. The stone here was erected in 1827. See 'The Killing Times' above.

Ochiltree Hill

From this grand viewpoint on the SUW, the Martyr's Monument on Windy Hill above Wigtown can be seen to the south-east. This obelisk honours all those who died unjustly during the Killing Times (see above) between 1662 and 1686, but particularly the 'Two Margarets', 63 year old Margaret McLaughlan and 18 year old Margaret Wilson, who were barbarously put to death for their faith by drowning on the incoming tide in Wigtown Bay. Wigtown is well worth a visit on a subsequent trip to south-west Scotland.

Bargrennan

This is a tiny settlement. The Reverend Dick (see Appendix 2) who passed this way at the time of the First World War noted that there was 'scarcely anything but the church, manse, school and post-office'. Alas the latter triplet have now gone, but the walker will welcome the old House o' Hill Hotel. Dick supposed that this famous old Inn received its name from an earlier building that once stood on the adjacent hill.

STAGE 4

Bargrennan to St John's Town of Dalry

24.3 miles (39.1km)

	Distance (miles)		Distance (km)	
	Sectional	Cumulative	Sectional	Cumulative
Bargrennan	0	40.1	0	64.5
Twin Bridges of Trool	4.2	44.3	6.7	71.2
Caldons	1.7	46.0	2.7	73.9
East end of Loch Trool	1.7	47.7	2.8	76.7
Loch Dee	3.4	51.1	5.5	82.2
Clatteringshaws Loch	4.7	55.8	7.5	89.7
Knocksheen	5.4	61.2	8.7	98.4
Waterside Hill (172m)	2.3	63.5	3.7	102.1
St John's Town of Dalry	0.9	64.4	1.5	103.6

Alternatives
Firstly a warning. The stage from Bargrennan to Dalry is a very long one, crossing remote country through the Galloway hills, with few roads and no facilities save a bothy at White Laggan about 18km (11.2 miles) from Bargrennan. Be sure to take adequate food and drink and an early start is essential in order to avoid being benighted, particularly outside the period between May and mid-August when the days are shorter. This stage is followed by an even longer one and only the fit and experienced should attempt these two consecutive days.

Stages 4 and 5 are given as stated in this guidebook because Bargrennan, Dalry and Sanquhar are the only places where accommodation and food and drink may be obtained on the route. However, those unsure of their ability to walk such long distances have a very feasible option. These two long stages can be broken down into three shorter sections that are more manageable to walk over a three-day period. If a friend cannot help with the necessary transport arrangements for this plan then help is on hand from a commercial company based in Dalry.

Southern Upland Way Ltd (**Southernuplandway.com**) offers vehicle support and baggage transfer services over the whole of the SUW, but they are of particular use in overcoming the long section between Bargrennan and Sanquhar. The company will pick up walkers near Clatteringshaws Loch after a walk of approximately 26.2km (16.3 miles) taking them to overnight accommodation in Dalry and returning them to the same point the next morning. The second day is spent walking from here via Dalry to Stroanpatrick, a distance of about 25.4km (15.8 miles). A second pick-up from here and another overnight in Dalry with a return journey back to Stroanpatrick the following morning, for the last stage to Sanquhar, a distance of around 30.5km (18.9 miles).

The vehicle 'Pick-Up Points' are identified by wooden plaques on SUW signposts (see under 'Route' for Stages 4 and 5). Details are as follows.

Pick-Up Point 1: Craigenbay (1km north of Clatteringshaws Loch, West of Dalry), grid reference NX 543789, usually at 5pm. Overnight accommodation in St John's Town of Dalry. Walkers are dropped off, usually at 9.30am, the next morning at Craigenbay. They are then collected that evening, usually at around 6pm, at **Pick-Up Point 2:** Stroanpatrick, grid reference NX 642918 on the B729, for another night in Dalry. The next morning, usually at 8.30pm, walkers are returned to Stroanpatrick for the now manageable section along the SUW to Sanquhar.

The first few miles of this stage from Bargrennan are completely different from the original line of the SUW, making this the most significant of the route realignments along the whole of the route from west to east coast. The original route was a fairly direct line on a forest track eastward to the Holm of Bargrennan, but it became unsuitable because of the intensity of commercial forestry operations and so was closed in 2001. A major new routing replaced it around the edge of the forest, following the banks of the River Cree and the Water of Minnoch. The new route is about 3.4km (2.1 miles) in length, longer than the original route, but a definite improvement on the original plod through the forest.

From time to time, usually during the wetter winter months, the River Cree and Water of Minnoch overflow their banks. Under these conditions the only safe and viable route is an alternative trail via Glentrool Village and Stroan Bridge Visitor Centre & Tea Room to the Twin Bridges of Trool where the standard route is joined. ▶

Details of this alternative route will be found on the SUW Information Board at the point where the SUW emerges onto the A714 at Bargrennan.

Summary

The stage starts with pleasant riverside walking following the River Cree, the Water of Minnoch and finally the Water of Trool to the western end of Loch Trool. From here the Way passes between the Galloway Hills, firstly on a steeply undulating path above the loch, amongst trees but with many glimpses of the loch and surrounding mountains. There follows another relatively new section of the SUW, up an open hillside on an ancient path that provides some of the best views on all of the Southern Upland Way. The effort of the climb on this new mountain path route is rewarded with superb mountain views.

Loch Trool

To the north lies Merrick, the highest hill in Scotland outside the Highlands, and the large wilderness area of the Ridge of the Awful Hand; to the north-east is the Corbett of Corserine topping the Rhinns of Kells mountain range, whilst to the south the giants of Lamachan and Curleywee will be seen. Although the ascent is wet and boggy in places, particularly after rain, the line of this new route of the SUW offers spectacular views and is a tremendous improvement on the original line, which followed the track through the trees seen below.

Easier walking follows on tracks for several miles, but the area is still highly scenic, passing Loch Dee with the possibility of a night in a bothy at White Laggan. More track walking leads to the very large Clatteringshaws Loch whose northern shore is followed for a short distance before the Way takes to the hills again. The route heads northwards for a while, first through forestry plantations and then over open hillsides beneath the mountain of Meikle Millyea on the southern edge of the Rhinns of Kells. An easy section follows, gradually descending on a track, then a minor road before tackling the 'sting in the tail' of this long stage, an ascent of Waterside Hill, from whose summit there is a bird's-eye view down to St John's Town of Dalry, your friendly destination for the night. This route over Waterside Hill is not the original line of the SUW, which went more to the south avoiding the hill. Again this is an improvement on the original route providing an excellent viewpoint, although weary long-distance walkers who have travelled all the way from Bargrennan in the day may think that Waterside was maybe just a 'hill too far'! Dalry is a veritable metropolis with all you may require in terms of a variety of accommodation, shops and pubs.

Route

From your place of lodging return to the SUW signpost on the A714 on the north side of the bridge over the River Cree. Take the delightful path alongside the east bank of this river. The path, which soon climbs above the river, is usually well maintained, which is fortunate, as if the extensive vegetation were not cut back frequently it would soon become overgrown.

Cross a minor road (stone bridge on right) and continue ahead.

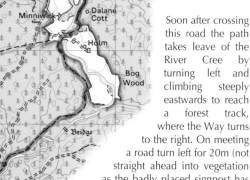

Map continues p. 72

Soon after crossing this road the path takes leave of the River Cree by turning left and climbing steeply eastwards to reach a forest track, where the Way turns to the right. On meeting a road turn left for 20m (not straight ahead into vegetation as the badly placed signpost has encouraged many people to do!) and then turn right onto a gravel track. Leave the track after five minutes or so onto a thin waymarked path, now alongside the **Water of Minnoch.** This lovely woodland path meanders north-east along the north-western bank of the river, through open glades offering views of the surrounding Forest Park and the Galloway Hills, before crossing a high stone stile, re-entering woodland and turning north-westwards. Soon after the white buildings of Holm are seen over the river to the right the trail crosses a footbridge and resumes the original line of the SUW at a track.

Turn right to cross the bridge over the River Minnoch. Jimmy Macgregor was here for filming when the SUW opened in 1984. The nearby 'Poachers' Road' is renowned as a favourite haunt of otters. Turn immediately left on a path with the river now on your left. The path follows this very picturesque stretch of river to reach a Water of Trool Information Board at a path junction. This is the Twin Bridges of Trool where those who chose the alternative route via **Glentrool Village** and **Stroan Bridge** Visitor Centre & Tea Room will re-join the SUW. Turning left here would take you to a footbridge over the river, but the SUW continues ahead, now following the south bank of the Water of Trool. The mighty Galloway Hills dominate the landscape hereabouts. A good path, which the SUW shares with a local route (yellow

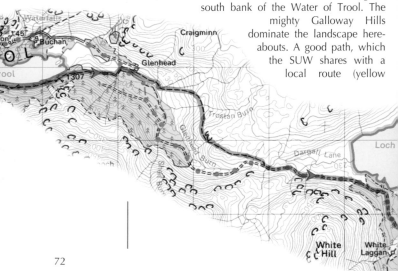

stripe waymarks), leads up **Glen Trool** to the site of Caldons Camp Site, now sadly closed, at the western end of Loch Trool.

The SUW now heads along a grassy and wooded area to the south of Loch Trool. Follow the signpost for the SUW and Loch Trool Trail alongside the Water of Trool. After an initial flat section the forest trail climbs high above the loch, which is eventually seen down to the left. The path then descends almost to the lochside. This is quite a steeply undulating and rather exhausting path, but it does provide good views of the loch and the mountains that tower above the water, as it and you make your way to the east end of the loch. The Trail, alas, then climbs even higher as it continues to a SUW Information Board and footbridge.

From this point the original route of the Southern Upland Way took to the track here, a rather mundane plod to Loch Dee. However the new and much improved line of the Way makes use of an old footpath over open hillside to the north-east and so doing provides excellent views back to Loch Trool, to the Merrick and other Hills of the Galloway Forest Park. If weather

Map continues p. 76

73

The eastern end of Loch Trool

conditions are dire then the wise would opt for the original track route, but otherwise the new route of the SUW is much to be recommended. Cross the footbridge and turn right along a riverside path. Cross a track opposite the buildings of **Glenhead**. Cross a stile and then a boulder-strewn stream to head uphill to the left as indicated by a SUW waymarker post. The effort of the climb is rewarded with spectacular mountain views.

Just before joining the track of the original route **Loch Dee** comes into view to the east. Descend to the track (SUW Information Board) and turn left along it. Some easy walking follows, but you are in most impressive hill country. The track offers good views of Loch Dee before it enters trees and descends to cross **White Laggan Burn**. White Laggan Bothy (see Appendix 1) can be seen to the south, about 0.5km (0.3 mile) off-route, reached by a good grassy path, leaving the SUW on the right. It would be a haven in severe weather conditions, providing perhaps shelter whilst lunch is enjoyed out of the rain, or even for an overnight stay.

The SUW track climbs above and traverses the south-east shore of Loch Dee offering fine views into the remote hills of Craignaw (645m; 2116ft) and Dungeon Hill (620m; 2034 ft). Look out for a bench on the left of the track at a good viewpoint into these hills. The track climbs and then descends again to reach a track T-junction at an 'S' bend. Turn left down the track, which leads to a bridge over the Black Water of Dee. A few metres after this bridge bear right on a track (no waymark) and shortly, when this reaches another track T-junction, bear right again. Remain on this track for almost 4km to reach Clatteringshaws Loch. The large dome of the Cairnsmore or Black Craig of Dee (493m; 1617ft) will be seen ahead (to the east-south-east) in the distance whilst on this walk. When you reach a large clearing be sure to look back at the dramatic crags of Cairngarroch (557m; 1827ft). The track eventually passes under high-tension electricity cables and soon afterwards the huge expanse of water that is **Clatteringshaws Loch** comes into view.

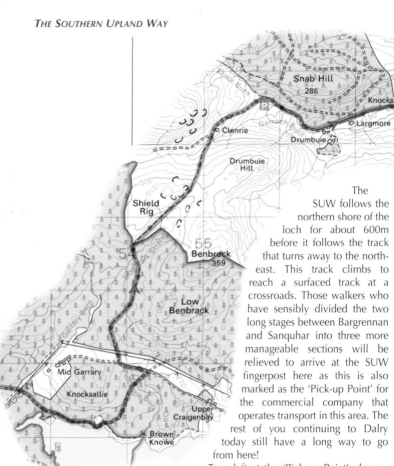

The SUW follows the northern shore of the loch for about 600m before it follows the track that turns away to the north-east. This track climbs to reach a surfaced track at a crossroads. Those walkers who have sensibly divided the two long stages between Bargrennan and Sanquhar into three more manageable sections will be relieved to arrive at the SUW fingerpost here as this is also marked as the 'Pick-up Point' for the commercial company that operates transport in this area. The rest of you continuing to Dalry today still have a long way to go from here!

Turn left at the 'Pick-up Point' along a track for about 500m. At a SUW fingerpost turn right over a wooden stile to follow a path along a dry stone wall (dyke). Cross another stile, where SUW Leaflet Boxes should be found, and follow the path into a forestry plantation. The Trail climbs through firebreaks in the forestry, eventually emerging on the open fellside and traversing Shield Rig. This is on the very edge of the Rhinns of Kells,

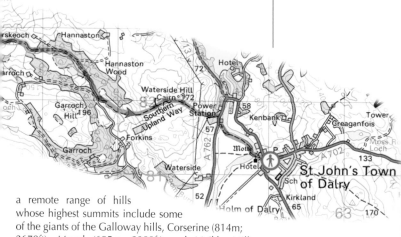

a remote range of hills
whose highest summits include some
of the giants of the Galloway hills, Corserine (814m;
2670ft), Meaul (695m; 2280ft) and Meikle Millyea
(746m; 2447ft). The steep slopes of the latter rise up to
the north-west of Shield Rig and dominate the view in
this area. ▶ Soon after passing some large boulders, a
grand view of the distant hills opens out. The path over
the moorland then begins to improve and descends to
reach a track at the solitary house of **Clenrie**.

The terrain is stony
hereabouts and often
overgrown, so take
especial care not to
stumble.

All is now plain sailing for a while as the track
descends to the edge of the forestry plantation below Snab
Hill, then turning to skirt the boundary of these trees,
heading south-eastwards. At the building of **Drumbuie** the
track runs into a narrow metalled lane, which is followed
in an easterly direction towards Dalry. Descend gradually
on this quiet lane, passing the farm of **Knocksheen**, for a
little under 4km until, soon after the lane crosses a bridge,
and with the river now on your left, look out for a SUW
fingerpost on the left-hand side of the lane.

This signpost directs the walker onto a path that runs
alongside the river to meet and cross a footbridge. Cross
a ladder stile and summon up the strength for one last
climb of the stage, up **Waterside Hill**. The route of the
SUW goes close to the top of the hill, but strangely

77

doesn't visit the actual summit. So a short detour is required to reach the summit cairn at the high point of 172m (564ft). There is a grand panorama from here, from the high hills in the north including the giant Cairnsmore of Carsphairn (797m; 2614ft) to those in the north-west (Corserine), and west (Meikle Millyea). But the most welcome site to the weary walker will be the houses of the picturesque village of **St John's Town of Dalry** nestling below the hillside.

Follow the SUW waymarker posts from the little col below the summit of Waterside Hill down towards the village (there is often almost head high bracken on this hillside during the summer months, which rather spoils the experience). The Trail leads to a road by a 'water ladder'. Turn right for 20m and then left through a kissing gate to gain access onto a path alongside the river. Cross the large suspension bridge to enter Dalry near its church, passing a SUW Information Board on the ascent from the bridge to the main road. The Way emerges onto Dalry High Street next to the Clachan Inn, the home of **southernuplandway.com**.

Clachan Inn and Church, St John's Town of Dalry

PLACES OF INTEREST

Galloway Forest Park
Much of the area between Dalmellington and Girvan in the north and Newton Stewart and New Galloway in the south is now the Galloway Forest Park, a huge area of high mountain, moorland, lochs and commercial forestry covering 240 square miles. ▶ There are Visitor Centres at Kirroughtree and Clatteringshaws Loch.

Apart from the long-distance SUW that passes right through the Park, there are a number of short marked walking trails, cycling routes and forest drives.

Caldons
Until a few years ago there was a pleasant and useful campsite here, much used by SUW walkers. In the nearby Caldons Wood there is a martyr's tomb which bears witness to the murder of six Covenanters who were surprised at prayer and immediately shot here by one Colonel Douglas in 1685.

Galloway Hills
The Galloway Hills are a very extensive range of mountains that contain some twenty-six hills over 2000 feet in height, as well as three of the seven Corbetts of southern Scotland, Shalloch on Minnoch (775m; 2542ft), Corserine (814m; 2670ft), and the highest point in southern Scotland, Merrick (843m; 2765ft). Whilst the latter mountain has a path to the summit and is relatively easy of access, this is not the case with the majority of the range, whose hills are often remote and exceedingly rough, testing the skill of the seasoned hillwalker and backpacker.

The North Galloway Hills consist of three ranges, the Rhinns of Carsphairn, the Rhinns of Kells (Rhinns in this sense comes from the Gaelic word 'rinn' which means a sharp point) and the rocky Dungeon range to the east. The ridges to the west are said to resemble that of a gigantic hand and thus are known, rather dramatically, as the Range of the Awful Hand. The main hills in the North Galloway Hills are Merrick (843m; 2765ft), Shalloch on Minnoch (775m; 2542ft), Craignaw (645m; 2116ft), Dungeon Hill (610m; 2001ft), Mullwharchar (692m; 2270ft), Meikle Millyea (746m; 2447ft), Corserine (814m; 2670ft), Carlin's

Cairn (807m; 2647ft), Cairnsgarroch (659m; 2280ft) and Coran of Portmark (623m; 2043ft). The South Galloway Hills consist of the Lamachans or Minnigaff Hills, Larg Hill (676m; 2217ft), Lamachan Hill (716m; 2349ft), Curleywee (674m; 2207ft) and Millfore (665m; 2181ft) as well as numerous scattered isolated summits, including Cairnsmore of Fleet (711m; 2332ft), Criffel (569m; 1866ft), Bengairn (391m; 1282ft) and Screel Hill (343m; 1125ft).

Loch Trool

A much-visited beauty spot, situated at the head of Glentrool, surrounded by pine trees and the rugged mountains of the Galloway Hills. It is over 2km long but no more than 400m at its widest points. The lochside is the site of the historic Battle of Glen Trool where in 1307 at the steep-sided Steps of Trool (grid reference NX 422797) the English were routed by Robert the Bruce's forces. The battle is commemorated by the Bruce Memorial Stone, a gigantic boulder above the loch on the opposite side to that used by the SUW. The area of hill and moorland between Loch Trool and Loch Dee to the east is the site of the famous supposed chase in John Buchan's novel *The Thirty-Nine Steps*.

Clatteringshaws Loch

A very extensive area of water, over 3km long and over 2km wide at its widest, northern, end. The loch is a reservoir, formed by the damming of the River Dee. The area is known for its wild goats, and deer are not uncommon hereabouts. On the opposite shore to that used by the SUW there is an interesting Visitor Centre detailing some local history and having a reconstruction of an ancient hut dwelling. Nearby is a Bruce's Stone commemorating another victory over the English, again in the year 1307. The Levellers, the people's champions of their day (the 17th century), were active in this area. Clatteringshaws Loch is popular with car tourists, offering easy access by the A712, good car parking and an attractive Forest Drive along the 'Raiders Road' from Clatteringshaws to the A762 south of New Galloway near Loch Ken.

Clatteringshaws Loch

St John's Town of Dalry

Known locally merely as 'Dalry' (from the Gaelic *dail righ*, 'meadow of the king') the town is said to have been given its full title by the Knights Templar. The picturesque town is the principal one in the district of the Glenkens, the valley drained by the Water of Ken, from Carsphairn in the north to the attractive Loch Ken in the south, a popular spot with tourists and anglers. In recent years red kites have been very successfully introduced into the Glenkens and it is possible to see these birds, particularly from the various viewing areas near Loch Ken and at the Kite Feeding Station near Laurieston, both on the 'Galloway Kite Trail'. Dalry was a seat of unrest for the Covenanters of the 17th century and several of them are buried in the churchyard. Nowadays it has become a centre for walking in the area, hosting a major business catering for SUW hikers, walker-friendly accommodation and a new walking trail down the valley to New Galloway. Grocery shops, pubs, hotels, B&Bs and a post office are all to be found in friendly Dalry.

The high street is a very steep one, as SUW walkers will soon discover on setting out for the next stage of their journey. At the top end of the village is found a block of stone shaped like a seat. Tradition has it that John the Baptist rested here! Be sure to look at this and the view of the Rhinns of Kells above Dalry before taking your leave.

STAGE 5

St John's Town of Dalry to Sanquhar

26.7 miles (43km)

| | Distance (miles) | | Distance (km) | |
	Sectional	Cumulative	Sectional	Cumulative
St John's Town of Dalry	0	64.4	0	103.6
Ardoch	1.9	66.3	3.0	106.6
Butterhole Bridge	3.2	69.5	5.2	111.8
Stroanpatrick	2.7	72.2	4.3	116.1
Manquhill Hill (421m)	2.4	74.6	3.8	119.9
Benbrack (580m)	2.0	76.6	3.3	123.2
Black Hill (568m)	1.5	78.1	2.4	125.6
Allan's Cairn	1.2	79.3	2.0	127.6
Polskeoch Bothy	2.0	81.3	3.3	130.9
Polgown	3.2	84.5	5.1	136.0
Cloud Hill	1.6	86.1	2.6	138.6
Sanquhar	5.0	91.1	8.0	146.6

Summary
This is the longest and perhaps hardest of all the stages on the SUW and is again through remote country, with very long sections between roads and no opportunity to acquire extra provisions or obtain a bed for the night without a lengthy detour off-route. The same warning applies as for Stage 4, but also bear in mind the possibility of even greater fatigue after the exertions of yesterday. There is though the possibility of cutting the day short by arranging transport to pick you up at Stroanpatrick (see under 'Alternatives' in Stage 4). Another option is to rest at the youth hostel at Kendoon which is 2.5km off-route, but this is really too early in the day to save much distance the following day. Those with sleeping bags and sufficient food can break the journey very conveniently at lovely Polskeoch bothy.

Careful navigation over moorland is required on this stage particularly on the first section from Dalry to Stroanpatrick. The route is waymarked with wooden marker posts over these areas, but in 2005 they were very old (probably the originals, dating from 1984), often difficult to locate and infrequently spaced.

The stage starts with a cross-country section via Ardoch Hill and Butterhole Bridge that requires concentration to stay on the correct line, as the trail is often over pathless grassy moorland terrain, any paths there tending to be thin, but they are usually non-existent. A compass is very useful as it would be wise not to lose the route, and therefore time and wasted energy, here as the day is a long one, if planning to walk the whole stage to Sanquhar. After Stroanpatrick Farm the trail heads uphill into remote upland country, generally on good paths, first over Manquhill Hill followed by a long, steep climb up to the highest point reached on the SUW to date, the summit of Benbrack (580m; 1902ft), from where there is an excellent 360 degree panorama of the surrounding high Galloway hills. Some walking through forestry

Inside the excellent Polskeoch Bothy

plantations leads to Polskeoch, possibly the most well-kept and well-presented bothy anywhere in Scotland. But perhaps the real highlight of this section of the SUW comes in the latter stages of the walk, the last 8km or so, after the route leaves a minor road and makes a beeline over the hills to Sanquhar. This walk offers first-rate views of the Southern Upland hills with its deeply gouged valleys, and in its latter stages presents the delightful scene of the town of Sanquhar nestling cosily in rural Nithsdale. Hopefully the long-distance walker will be not be too tired after this, the longest stage of the SUW, to enjoy the facilities on offer in the town.

With the long descent into Sanquhar, Galloway is finally left behind as one enters the north-western half of the old county of Dumfriesshire, which was technically abolished in the county reorganisations of the mid-1970s, but which is still very much alive in the minds of locals, as are the old counties of Wigtownshire, the Stewartry, Peeblesshire and the other former counties through which the SUW passes. ▶ The SUW now commences a complete traverse of Dumfriesshire until Scottish Borders Region is entered at Ettrick Head after Moffat.

Even if ignored by the Post Office the people who live in southern Scotland will often give their addresses with pride as Dumfriesshire or Wigtownshire or Peeblesshire, or whatever was their old county.

Route

Leave **Dalry** by taking the road opposite the church and the Clachan Inn, signposted to Moniaive (A702). Walk up the Main Street to the top of the hill. Shortly after the B7000, which turns off to the left and which you ignore, bear left off the main road onto a minor road which soon becomes a grassy track, leaving the last houses of the village behind. Follow SUW waymarker posts carefully across several grassy fields linked by ladder stiles, to pass to the left of the farm of Ardoch, after which the trail skirts to the east of **Ardoch Hill**. Some concentration is required to follow the SUW waymarks along this section, where the route on the ground is often invisible and the marker posts not as frequent at times as one would hope. A bridge is crossed and the route heads north-north-east, then north-north-west and finally north to reach a minor

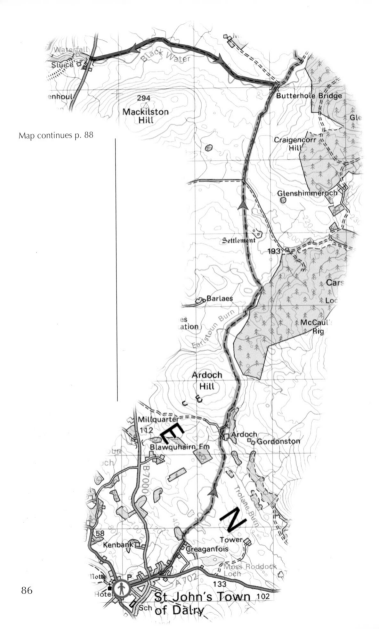

Waterfall

Sluice

Black Water

enhoul

294

Mackilston Hill

Butterhole Bridge

Gle

Craigencorr Hill

Map continues p. 88

Glenshimmeroch

Settlement

193

Cars

Barlaes

Loc

Earlstoun Burn

es ation

McCaul Rig

Ardoch Hill

Millquarter

112

Blawquhairn Fm

Ardoch

Gordonston

B7000

58

Troloss Burn

Kenbank

Tower

Creaganfois

Moss Roddock Loch

Notte

P

Hotel

A 702

133

102

St John's Town of Dalry

Sch

86

road at a crossroads (grid reference NX 637868). Particular care is required not to come off-route on this section by taking the path that leads from the farm of Barlaes to 'point 193' on the road (refer to the Ordnance Survey map). ▶ The waymarker posts in this area, which are important guides in keeping to the correct line of the Way, are probably over twenty years old. At the time of the author's research they were in some need of restoration, and ideally more posts should be erected at crucial points. It is a good idea to follow the compass carefully during this crossing.

If this error is inadvertently made then simply walk north-north-west on the road until you meet the road junction (grid reference NX 637868) where the true line of the SUW is rejoined.

On reaching the aforementioned road junction cross the cattle grid and walk northwards on the lane to **Butterhole Bridge**. On the far side of this bridge an official SUW detour on the left will take those staying at Kendoon Youth Hostel to their overnight accommodation. It is a walk of about 2.5km off-route. But the SUW continues ahead on the road for a further 300m to another SUW fingerpost, where the path is taken

Stroanpatrick Farm

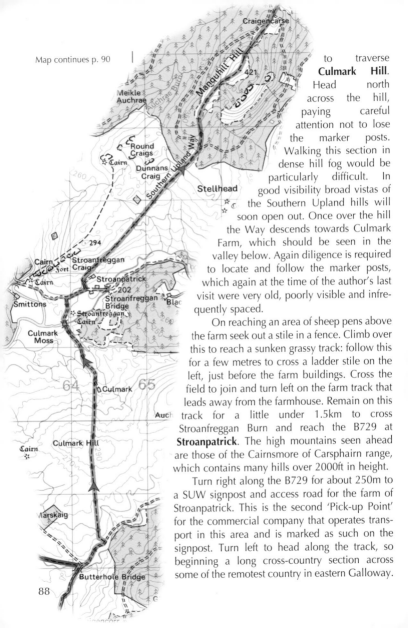

Map continues p. 90

to traverse **Culmark Hill**. Head north across the hill, paying careful attention not to lose the marker posts. Walking this section in dense hill fog would be particularly difficult. In good visibility broad vistas of the Southern Upland hills will soon open out. Once over the hill the Way descends towards Culmark Farm, which should be seen in the valley below. Again diligence is required to locate and follow the marker posts, which again at the time of the author's last visit were very old, poorly visible and infrequently spaced.

On reaching an area of sheep pens above the farm seek out a stile in a fence. Climb over this to reach a sunken grassy track: follow this for a few metres to cross a ladder stile on the left, just before the farm buildings. Cross the field to join and turn left on the farm track that leads away from the farmhouse. Remain on this track for a little under 1.5km to cross Stroanfreggan Burn and reach the B729 at **Stroanpatrick**. The high mountains seen ahead are those of the Cairnsmore of Carsphairn range, which contains many hills over 2000ft in height.

Turn right along the B729 for about 250m to a SUW signpost and access road for the farm of Stroanpatrick. This is the second 'Pick-up Point' for the commercial company that operates transport in this area and is marked as such on the signpost. Turn left to head along the track, so beginning a long cross-country section across some of the remotest country in eastern Galloway.

Many miles have to be trekked before the next metalled road is encountered at Polskeoch. Leave the track at a marker post just before a gate (note that electric fencing crossed this track at the time of the author's visit). Follow the path up the hillside behind the farm. Once again some care is required in following the thistle waymarker posts, particularly at first, but the path later becomes more obvious as it approaches forestry. Cross a forest track to follow a path along a firebreak in the plantation. Fortunately the route is out of the trees for the most part as it traverses **Manquhill** (pronounced 'Manwill') Hill (421m; 1381ft) offering excellent mountain views to the north and west. The most prominent hills are Cairnsmore of Carsphairn (797m; 2614ft), Windy Standard (688m; 2257ft) and Blackcraig Hill (700m; 2296ft). The pylons of the extensive wind farm on the slopes of Windy Standard should be visible to the north-west on a clear day.

A good path provides a gentle descent of Manquhill Hill, with the giant of Benbrack, your next objective, looming ahead. Cross an old forest track, pass between two ponds and cross another track before beginning the ascent. After a false summit the true top of **Benbrack** (580m; 1902ft) is reached at a triangulation pillar (OS number plate S8223). ▶ Cairnsmore of Carsphairn and Windy Standard dominate the view to the west, whilst to the north the tops of Alhang (642m; 2106ft), Alwhat (628m; 2060ft) and Blackcraig Hill are seen to good effect.

A 360-degree view rewards your efforts in climbing to the highest point reached on the SUW since leaving Portpatrick.

Bear north-west and soon north off the summit of Benbrack along the northern ridge of the hill. **Black Hill** (568m; 1863ft), the next objective, is reached in just under 3km of walking on the open grassy hillside. A further kilometre of walking along the forest plantation leads to **High Countam** (about 500m; 1640ft). The Way then heads north-east into the trees to cross a forest track and continues to reach **Allan's Cairn** (497m; 1630ft), where there is a memorial stone to the martyrs Margaret Gracie and George Allan. Bear to the left at this point to follow a path that meanders through the forest, eventually arriving at a track. Turn right here, following the

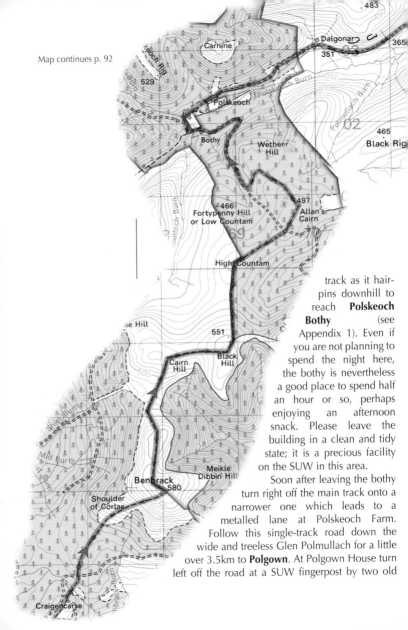

Map continues p. 92

track as it hairpins downhill to reach **Polskeoch Bothy** (see Appendix 1). Even if you are not planning to spend the night here, the bothy is nevertheless a good place to spend half an hour or so, perhaps enjoying an afternoon snack. Please leave the building in a clean and tidy state; it is a precious facility on the SUW in this area.

Soon after leaving the bothy turn right off the main track onto a narrower one which leads to a metalled lane at Polskeoch Farm. Follow this single-track road down the wide and treeless Glen Polmullach for a little over 3.5km to **Polgown**. At Polgown House turn left off the road at a SUW fingerpost by two old sandstone gateposts. The SUW now makes a beeline for Sanquhar, but it is several more miles before the town and your night's rest is achieved. The path leaves Polgown and first climbs the shoulder of Rough Hill. Grand views of rolling hills and long flat grassy ridges soon unfold. The route passes over **Cloud Hill** (451m; 1479ft) from where there is a fine view of the hills and valleys to the south-east: the rocks of Glenwhargen Craig are particularly outstanding.

After a seemingly endless climb, the high point of the path is reached, so beginning the long descent into Sanquhar, which soon comes into view below. This last section of the day provides one of the most memorable views of the entire SUW, the long, slow drop down to Sanquhar in Nithsdale with the houses of the town in view all the way. When about a couple of kilometres from Sanquhar bear right at a SUW marker post to cross a river by a large wooden footbridge. More marker posts lead the walker to a gravel track: follow this to a lane at

Blackaddie Hotel, Sanquhar

the farm buildings of Ulzieside. Turn left onto the road to cross the river (Eachan Water). At the junction turn right to pass over a second bridge, this one built in 1855, over the River Nith.

On the far side of the river turn right onto a minor road beside the river. There is a SUW Information Board and picnic tables here, but the tired walker will probably wish to reach his or her night's accommodation at this stage in the day, rather than linger awhile at this attractive spot. Remain on this lane to pass a 20mph speed sign, so entering the town. The lane leads to the High Street (A76) in **Sanquhar**. Turn left for the Blackaddie House Hotel or right for the centre of town and the campsite. Note that this final approach to Sanquhar is a shorter route than the original line of the SUW, which took a path to the south of Sanquhar to arrive at the A76 at the south-east end of the town.

PLACES OF INTEREST

Ardoch Farm
This property is associated with the Covenanters. During the Killing Times Robert Stewart, a Covenanter of Ardoch, was involved in the

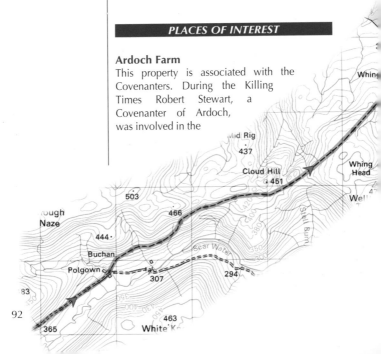

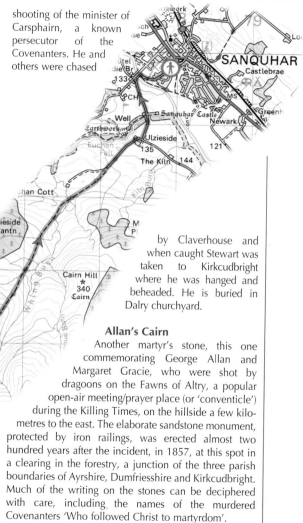

shooting of the minister of Carsphairn, a known persecutor of the Covenanters. He and others were chased by Claverhouse and when caught Stewart was taken to Kirkcudbright where he was hanged and beheaded. He is buried in Dalry churchyard.

Allan's Cairn

Another martyr's stone, this one commemorating George Allan and Margaret Gracie, who were shot by dragoons on the Fawns of Altry, a popular open-air meeting/prayer place (or 'conventicle') during the Killing Times, on the hillside a few kilometres to the east. The elaborate sandstone monument, protected by iron railings, was erected almost two hundred years after the incident, in 1857, at this spot in a clearing in the forestry, a junction of the three parish boundaries of Ayrshire, Dumfriesshire and Kirkcudbright. Much of the writing on the stones can be deciphered with care, including the names of the murdered Covenanters 'Who followed Christ to martyrdom'.

Sanquhar Post Office, Britain's oldest

Sanquhar

This town on the River Nith is famous as the home of Britain's oldest post office, established in 1763, when 'post boys' delivered mail on horseback. It is possible that it is also the oldest continuously used post office in the world, although there is some doubt about this claim. It is an unassuming building in the High Street, and now doubles as a Tourist Information Centre. The Tolbooth Museum, also in the High Street, has an interesting collection focusing on local history. The High Street is also the location for the Richard Cameron Monument. Cameron was a Covenanter who, in 1680, posted on the old town cross which stood on this spot the 'Sanquhar Declaration' which laid out his grievances with the government over religious freedom. He paid with his life for this audacity.

The other building of note in Sanquhar (pronounced 'San-ker') is the old castle, now in ruins. Dating from the 14th century, it was acquired in the 17th century by the first Duke of Queensberry of Drumlanrig Castle. The latter is one of Scotland's great stately homes, home of the present Duke of Buccleuch, one of Britain's largest landowners. Lying about 9 miles south of Sanquhar off the A76, a visit to Drumlanrig would make an excellent day off from the SUW, provided transport can be arranged from Sanquhar.

One of Sanquhar's notable sons was the scholar and adventurer James Crichton, known famously as 'The Admirable Crichton'. Born in 1572 it is said that he could speak a dozen languages, but, alas, he died in a sword fight at the very early age of twenty-two years. Sanquhar was traditionally a centre for glove making, providing gloves for, amongst other notables, Mary Queen of Scots and Sir Winston Churchill. The SUW leaves the town by way of Cow Wynd. The seemingly rather strange name for a small street comes from the fact that in days past the town's cattle were led daily by this route out onto the moors for pasture: the original spelling was 'Coo Wynd'.

Sanquhar has all the facilities necessary to feed and accommodate the visitor.

STAGE 6

Sanquhar to Wanlockhead

7.4 miles (11.9km)

| | Distance (miles) | | Distance (km) | |
	Sectional	Cumulative	Sectional	Cumulative
Sanquhar	0	91.1	0	146.6
Cogshead	4.0	95.1	6.4	153.0
Meadowfoot	2.5	97.6	4.1	157.1
Wanlockhead	0.9	98.5	1.4	158.5

Summary
Today's route enters the Lowther Hills east of Sanquhar, taking in some of the lower hills of the range; it is not until after Wanlockhead that the Way traverses the very highest hills in the Lowthers. Sanquhar to Wanlockhead is a gem of a section over lofty rolling hills that are deeply riven by steep-sided valleys, to descend into the Wanlock valley, an area once famous, some would say infamous, for its lead mining industry. It is a short stage of less than 12km (7.5 miles), but most will find this a welcome respite from the two ultra-long stages that have preceded it. There is also much to see and do in Wanlockhead, in particular a visit to the Lead Mining Museum being thoroughly recommended. In order to do this justice a full afternoon is required, so today's short stage fits in well with this itinerary. Aim to reach Wanlockhead by lunchtime, and after settling into your accommodation, spend the afternoon at the museum.

As an alternative, if transport can be arranged (it is commercially available), the first part of the next stage, over the high Lowther Hills from Wanlockhead to the A702 at Overfingland, can be accomplished during the afternoon, so providing a much shorter and more

manageable stage on the morrow. The transport that will be required for this option is a pick-up from the A702 at Overfingland at the end of the day, back to your accommodation in Wanlockhead, and a return to this point after breakfast the next morning.

Tombstones and Yew trees, Wanlockhead Cemetery

Route

Walk south-east along the whole length of **Sanquhar** High Street, the A76, passing Britain's oldest post office, until just after the public library. Turn left along Cow Wynd. Pass over the railway line to begin a climb of over 1000ft (300m) onto the moors to the north-east of Sanquhar. Climb a steep grassy sward passing several benches, which can be used to rest and admire the view back down to Sanquhar. Bear right onto a gravel track to continue the climb. Where this track swings sharp right to Lochside Farm continue ahead at a large boulder. The trail over the moors levels and eventually leads to a minor road a couple of kilometres from Sanquhar. Turn

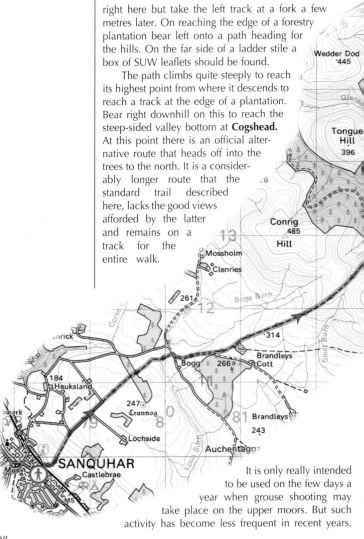

right here but take the left track at a fork a few metres later. On reaching the edge of a forestry plantation bear left onto a path heading for the hills. On the far side of a ladder stile a box of SUW leaflets should be found.

The path climbs quite steeply to reach its highest point from where it descends to reach a track at the edge of a plantation. Bear right downhill on this to reach the steep-sided valley bottom at **Cogshead.** At this point there is an official alternative route that heads off into the trees to the north. It is a considerably longer route that the standard trail described here, lacks the good views afforded by the latter and remains on a track for the entire walk.

It is only really intended to be used on the few days a year when grouse shooting may take place on the upper moors. But such activity has become less frequent in recent years.

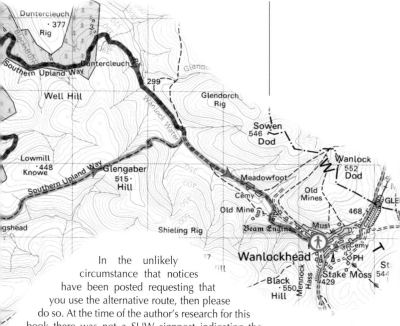

In the unlikely circumstance that notices have been posted requesting that you use the alternative route, then please do so. At the time of the author's research for this book there was not a SUW signpost indicating the alternative route at Cogshead; it appears that this route is seldom used.

To continue the standard trail turn right over a stile to start the climb out of this valley and over the hill towards Wanlockhead. The highest point, at around 480m (1574ft), is marked by a fieldgate and stile, after which it is all downhill on a grassy track. The valley is disfigured by numerous old disused lead mining sites. The SUW crosses the valley river, Wanlock Water, by a large wooden footbridge, in front of just one of these sites. The alternative route, that has remained on a track to the north of our route, meets the standard Way here at a SUW fingerpost on the main track that runs along the valley floor. Turn right (south-east) on this track heading for the highest village in Britain.

Wanlockhead

The track becomes metalled at Wanlockhead Sewage Treatment Works and passes the terrace of houses at **Meadowfoot**. Next pass the small but interesting Wanlockhead Cemetery, dating from the early 18th century, with its display of ancient yew trees, before making the gentle ascent into Wanlockhead village. Just before reaching the first houses the SUW turns right off the road to pass by some old mine workings and spoil heaps. Bear left in front of an enormous spoil heap of Matterhorn proportions, once more heading towards the village, but this time on the opposite side of the valley to the road. The Way finally reaches the heart of **Wanlockhead** at the entrance to the Lead Mining Museum.

PLACES OF INTEREST

Cogshead
The site of a ruined farmhouse. It is said that it is possible to see the area where peat was dug for fuel on the hill nearby. At nearby Martyr's Knowe three Covenanters captured by government troops escaped from them during a thunderstorm.

Wanlockhead
Wanlockhead, at 425m (1394ft), is Britain's highest village. It lies north of the dramatic Mennock Pass (southern Scotland's 'Glencoe'), in the heart of the Lowther Hills. Lead (galena or lead sulphide) was first discovered here by the Romans and for 250 years until the 1950s it was the focus of Scotland's lead mining industry, operated mainly by the Duke of Buccleuch. A great deal of this is still very much in evidence today, in the form of old mine workings, equipment, mine shafts and spoil heaps, a landscape despoliation that will sadden the hearts of many who enter the Wanlock valley.

At its height in the 19th century the population of the village was around 800, but it is considerably less today. However, once again Wanlockhead is prospering as it is home to a very successful tourist industry based on its justly famous Lead Mining Museum, and its properties are being actively sought by relatively wealthy 'incomers' who wish to enjoy the superb hill scenery that abounds and are not dissuaded by its rather exposed location and uncertain road access during severe winters.

A visit to the village usually centres on the Museum of Scottish Lead Mining, which was opened by Scottish celebrity Jimmy Macgregor on 7th August 1992. There is a display of rare minerals and mining artefacts, including working models of mining machinery, but the highlight is undoubtedly the guided tour of one of the lead mines. You can also try your hand at gold panning. The huge beam engine once used to pump water from the mines, a 'Bobbing John' which dates from the mid-19th century, is passed on the SUW and is the only reasonably

Wanlockhead Beam Engine

complete one remaining in the UK. Wanlockhead is also home to Europe's second oldest subscription library, containing over 3000 rare books. It dates from 1756 (the one in nearby Leadhills was opened in 1741 which makes it the oldest such library in Europe) and can be visited as part of the mining museum tour. There is a tearoom, which serves meals, and toilets at the main museum building. The museum is open daily from Easter or 1st April (whichever is earlier) to 31st October (admission charge).

Despite the success of Wanlockhead as a tourist village it is very sad that the SYHA hostel, which had the distinction of being one of the oldest and longest serving hostels in the SYHA, and certainly the highest in Scotland, closed permanently in the autumn of 2005. Fortunately it reopened in 2007 as an independent hostel affiliated to the SYHA.

STAGE 7

Wanlockhead to Beattock (Moffat)

20.5 miles (33km) + 1.3 miles (2.1km)

	Distance (miles)		Distance (km)	
	Sectional	Cumulative	Sectional	Cumulative
Wanlockhead	0	98.5	0	158.5
Lowther Hill (725m)	2.0	100.5	3.3	161.8
Cold Moss (628m)	1.2	101.7	1.9	163.7
Overfingland	2.1	103.8	3.3	167.0
Daer Reservoir	4.2	108.0	6.7	173.7
Hod's Hill (567m)	2.4	110.4	3.9	177.6
Brattleburn Bothy (turn-off path)	2.3	112.7	3.7	181.3
Earshaig	3.9	116.6	6.3	187.6
Beattock	2.4	119.0*	3.9	191.5*
Moffat	(1.3)	119.0*	(2.1)	191.5*

* Moffat is a 1.3 mile (2.1km) detour from the SUW. This distance is not added to the cumulative distance along the SUW.

Summary

Be sure to make an early start and take sufficient drink and provisions with you, as this section between Wanlockhead and Beattock is another long and hard walk, particularly if adding the extra mile into Moffat at the end. Most walkers will be forced to do just that, as there is no longer any accommodation in Beattock (except for campers), whereas Moffat has a large variety of hotels, guest houses and a campsite. In any case Moffat should definitely not be omitted from your itinerary, as it has much of interest. For those unwilling or unable to tackle such a long stage within one day there is help at hand. Some commercial outfits (enquire at local TICs or from **southernuplandway.com**) operate a transport service which enables SUW walkers to lengthen the short Stage 6 from Wanlockhead over the Lowther Hills to the A702 (making a total of 20.4km or 12.7 miles from Sanquhar to Overfingland on the A702) and therefore shorten Stage 7 by 8.5km (5.3 miles) to give a more manageable 24.5km or 15.2 miles from the A702 east of Lowther Hill to Moffat.

The Lowthers are the highest hills crossed on the whole of the SUW, the highest point reached on the Way being Lowther Hill at 725m (2378ft). This is not quite the very highest point of the Lowthers as this distinction is held by Green Lowther (732m; 2401ft), a summit that hill enthusiasts could easily reach by a mile detour along the high ridge north-east of Lowther Hill. Unlike most of the other ranges that the SUW crosses on its long journey from west to east coast, where the edges of the main hills are normally traversed, the Lowthers are taken on 'full frontal', with a high-level traverse of the central section of the range.

The first part of this long stage is a climb from Wanlockhead to the summit of Lowther Hill adorned with a white 'golf ball' communications device. The high Lowthers are traversed eastwards along a steeply undulating ridge over the summit of Cold Moss (628m; 2060ft), Comb Head (609m; 1998ft) and Laght Hill (507m; 1663ft) before finally descending to the A702 at Overfingland in the Potrail Valley. Mountain walkers will particularly appreciate this section of the SUW as it provides many extensive views of the surrounding deeply cut hills and steep-sided valleys that are so typical of the Southern Uplands. Well Hill and the Durisdeer range to the south are particularly well seen from this route, and walkers with time, either now or sometime in the future, are recommended to explore those hills.

After leaving the A702 the next section is dominated by the huge Daer Reservoir which frames the views of the mountain ranges hereabouts. There are good views back to the Lowther Hills in the east and over to the Moffat and Ettrick Hills to the west. Later a walk through forestry plantations leads to another of the bothies that serve the SUW, that of Brattleburn. More walking amongst trees is followed

Daer Reservoir

by a descent to the Evan Valley, the main communications artery of southern Scotland.

The technical end of the stage is at the village of Beattock, which, when there was a railway station here on the main line from Carlisle to Glasgow, was a thriving little community. Today it is greatly overshadowed by the larger town of Moffat, little more than a mile away, and it is to Moffat that most SUW walkers will gravitate. Moffat is one of major small tourist towns of southern Scotland, but it is still largely unspoilt and offers abundant accommodation to suit all tastes and wallets. A night in the town is insufficient to appreciate the area fully; it is the ideal place for a day's rest from the SUW.

Route

Starting from the Lead Mining Museum in **Wanlockhead,** climb the steps at the far side of the museum car park to take the path which crosses the road and follows the 'Public Footpath by the Enterkin Pass to Carronbridge' (signpost). The 'golf ball' on the summit of **Lowther Hill** is your target. Although Lowther Hill stands at 725m

(2378ft) above sea level the climb that one is faced with here to the summit is only of about 300m (1000ft), the advantage of starting from Britain's highest village. The path reaches and follows the radar station access road for a short distance before a SUW path leaves it on the right at a hairpin bend. This trail passes the road higher up the hill before the final pull up a grassy rake to the summit.

Keep the 'golf ball' over to your left at the summit area.

Descend south, then south-east from the top of Lowther Hill. Follow the waymarks that mainly, but not always, follow the fence line. From the col below Lowther Hill climb to the summit of **Cold Moss** (628m; 2060ft) and then continue along the ridge to Comb Head

(609m; 1998ft). A very steep descent follows, before an equally steep ascent of **Laght Hill** (507m; 1663ft). Strangely the Way does not quite reach the actual summit of this final hill, but follows the fence line along the ridge to the north-east. Cross a ladder stile and follow the path to the right of a wall and then a narrow belt of conifer trees that shield the farm of **Overfingland**, to descend to the A702.

Turn left along this road. Although an 'A' road, only light traffic will be encountered, a pleasant situation that is enjoyed on several of the main roads in both Dumfries & Galloway and the Borders. After about 800m, at a SUW fingerpost, turn right off the road. Do not follow the fence, but look for the first marker post half-left. Follow posts to a footbridge across the river (Potrail Water). A path from here leads to a track which is crossed (no waymarks here on my visit) and then on to a further track, which the SUW takes to the right, heading south-south-east. This soon leads to a fieldgate and stile at the edges of two plantations, with open hillside ahead. The track continues generally in an easterly direction, until eventually, after about 3km, a minor road is reached. Turn right, uphill, to reach the dam of **Daer Reservoir.**

Map continues p. 108

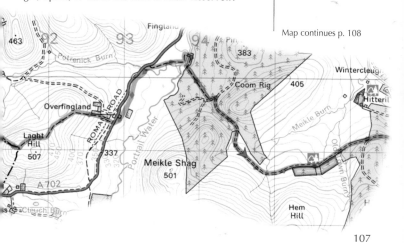

Turn left through a metal gate to walk across the dam, a distance of almost a kilometre. The original route of the SUW did not cross the dam, but went on a detour to the north-west before climbing **Sweetshaw Brae**. The new route over the dam is an improvement, being both shorter and offering better close-up views of this large stretch of water with the southern Lowther Hills rising up gracefully behind. Be sure to look back to see the 'golf ball' on the summit of Lowther Hill and the aerials on the top of Green Lowther.

After the completely flat dam comes a long climb eastwards up the rather charmingly named Sweetshaw Brae (448m; 1469ft) and then on to the summit of Hod's Hill (567m; 1860ft). Good views soon open out back to the west. From the high ground the Moffat Hills to the east, with the Corbett of mighty Hart Fell dominating, are now in prominent view, as is the shapely dome of Queensberry to the south-south-west. At spot height 567m on Hod's Hill the Way turns to the south-east to follow a fence to the corner of a forestry plantation. From here follow the edge of the plantation steeply down south-westwards to a col, from where there is an equally steep ascent up to the summit of **Beld Knowe** (507m; 1663ft). There are good views on the right during this section, down to Daer Reservoir and to the hills beyond.

Make the most of these, for the route is soon to plunge deep into forestry.

From Beld Knowe turn back to the south-east to follow the edge of the plantation for a further 400m or so before entering the forest on a path that descends along a wide firebreak down towards Mosshope. The Way eventually turns south, after which signs indicate the track to Brattleburn Bothy (see Appendix 1) off to the right. The bothy is about 300m off-route, and alas somewhat uphill, but a visit is worthwhile even if an overnight stop is not on your itinerary.

Map continues p. 110

Perhaps have a short rest and afternoon snack to summon up the resources for the last stretch of the Way to Beattock and Moffat.

After the bothy turn-off the SUW climbs through the forest to the top of **Craig Hill** (360m; 1181ft). Descend from this hill to cross two forest tracks in

*Roadside waymarker
on the SUW near
Easter Earshaig*

quick succession and continue ahead (south-south-east)
on a wide ride between plantations. The large farmstead
of Holmshaw is soon seen ahead in the distance across a
large clearing in the forest. Cross a wooden footbridge
over a burn, followed by a ladder stile, to enter this
clearing. Follow thistle waymarker posts across the
clearing to cross Foy's Bridge over the Garpol Burn.
Climb over another ladder stile to re-enter the trees to
the right (west) of **Holmshaw**. Ascend on another
wide forest ride. When the ground levels, a
good path allows easy walking through
the trees. At one point the SUW turns to
the right at a marker post (here differing
slightly from the original route). Walk
to the far end of the plantation and turn
left to walk with trees on your left and
open heathland on the right. Eventually
a local route (red stripe waymarks)
joins the SUW by coming in from the
right. Just before reaching a minor road
the Way passes a SUW Information
Board (Beattock Area) by a small,
delightful artificial lochan at Earshaig.

Turn left on this lane, which is known
locally as 'The Crooked Road', a little to the
east of the property of **Easter Earshaig**. A small

picnic area is soon reached, with an attractive marker stele indicating that it is 2.5 miles to Beattock. As the lane exits the Earshaigs Wood search for a small sandstone tablet on the left which tells of the tragic tale of one Ben Wilson of Holmshaw (the farm recently passed en route) who was killed by lightning hereabouts in August 1897. The single-track road crosses the open moorland of Beattock Hill (259m; 850ft), providing good views of the Ettrick and Moffat Hills before descending into the Evan Valley. The M74 motorway and the buildings of the village of Beattock should be easily identified below. The Evan Valley is the main line of communications in southern central Scotland, carrying both the main line Carlisle to Glasgow railway and the relatively new M74 motorway which succeeded the A74 as the main road north to the Central Belt and south to England.

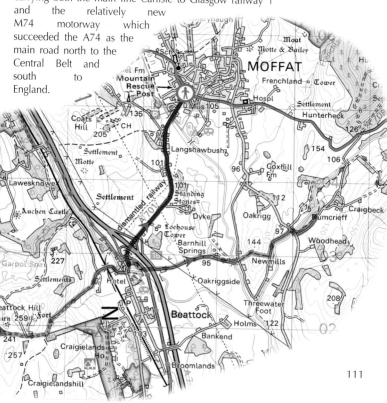

111

Pass over the railway on 'Bridge 193', continuing to reach a T-junction at Beattock. The main part of the village (campsite with bar and restaurant at Craigielands, but no other facilities) lies to the right, but for the SUW turn left towards a large roundabout near to the famous Telford built Old Brig Inn, now sadly not in use as a public house.

Most walkers will wish to visit the nearby town of Moffat for overnight accommodation, and this will mean leaving the Southern Upland Way at this point. After a stay in Moffat the walker has the choice of returning here to continue the Way (purists will no doubt take this option), or more sensibly leave Moffat on the minor road to Wamphray to pick up the official route a couple of kilometres further east. ◄

These routes are described at the start of Stage 8.

It is an easy and safe walk into Moffat from the Beattock Roundabout. Negotiate the roundabout by a series of pedestrian crossing points, controlled by traffic lights, pass under the M74 motorway and follow the A701 all the way into Moffat, a distance of about 2km. There is a pedestrian footpath along the right-hand side of this road all the way into the town. Those walkers not too exhausted by their efforts of the day are recommended a short visit to the Dyke Farm Nature Reserve, which is situated in the area of the old, now closed, Dyke Farm Quarry to the right of this road, before entering the town. The Reserve belongs to the Moffat and District Wildlife Club. There is a pond and wildlife hide, the area attracting in particular a large variety of birdlife. The Reserve is open to visitors as well as locals.

PLACES OF INTEREST

The Lowthers
The SUW has now entered the area of the central Southern Uplands, which consist principally of the Lowther, Moffat, Ettrick, Culter and Tweedsmuir Hills. The SUW passes through the first three of these ranges, although only on the Lowther Hills does it penetrate the heart of the hills. The main boundaries of the Lowthers

are the Nith valley to the west and the Annandale–
Evan–Clydesdale gap to the east. The highest summits of
Green Lowther (732m; 2401ft) and Lowther Hill (725m;
2378ft) are conspicuous for many a mile for they are
crowned by man-made objects, an array of large aerials
on the former, whilst Lowther Hill sports an enormous
white 'golf ball' radar station, which SUW walkers will
experience at close quarters. The highest point of the
SUW is here on Lowther Hill, not the actual top of the
hill, for this is occupied by the radar station, but a point
a few metres lower at around 720m (2362ft). ▶
The Enterkin Pass to the south of Lowther Hill was the
scene of several skirmishes between government troops
and Covenanters, most notable that of 1684 when a
group of Covenanters ambushed a group of dragoons
who gave up their Covenanter prisoners and fled. There
is fine walking to be had in this dramatic pass today on
Scottish Rights of Way (see the first and second refer-
ences in Appendix 2).

Other prominent hills in the range include East
Mount Lowther (631m; 2070ft), Dun Law (677m; 2221ft),
Ballencleuch Law (689m; 2260ft), Wedder Law (672m;
2204ft), Gana Hill (668m; 2191ft) and Queensberry
(697m; 2286ft). The latter is a very conspicuous hill on
the southern fringes of the range, towering above the
Forest of Ae, and is seen to good effect along the SUW,
particularly at Hod's Hill (567m; 1860ft).

Views are extensive
from up here; on
clear days they
extend as far afield
as the English Lake
District and the Isle
of Arran.

Daer Reservoir

Daer Reservoir, in a picturesque setting amongst the hills,
is over 3km long and almost 1.5km at its widest,
northern, end. The dam is 40m high and almost a kilometre long, the new route of the SUW crossing it. The
reservoir supplies approximately half of the water
requirements of Lanarkshire.

A little before Daer Reservoir on the route of the
SUW, the author found on his last visit a small notice
board pinned to a tree. It read: 'Daer Reservoir. Never in
the history of forestry so much done by so few'. And
some wag had added below it: 'For so few!'

Near Watermeetings Forest, a couple of miles before Daer Reservoir, the halfway point of the SUW will be passed. It is all downhill from here, as they say!

Beattock

Beattock's fortunes, and that of neighbouring Moffat, have waxed and waned over the years as communications along the Evan and Annandale valleys have fluctuated. In the 1820s a new road (today the old A74) was built from Beattock to Elvanfoot and the Road Commissioners' decision to have a hotel built at Beattock swung trade to the village and away from Moffat, which previously had been a major staging post. The resulting inn, a very fine building designed by Thomas Telford, a Dumfriesshire-born man, has been known variously over the years as the Lochhouse Hotel, the Beattock Inn and latterly the Old Brig Inn. The SUW passes the front of this famous building.

With the closure of the railway station, the building of the new M74 motorway and the increasing development of Moffat as a tourist destination, Beattock has today become something of a backwater. After years of struggling to be viable, the Old Brig Inn finally closed its doors to customers in 2005. ◀ It is still referred to as the Old Brig Inn in this guidebook, as this is how it is known locally. Beattock today offers excellent facilities for campers at Craigielands, but there is no other type of accommodation, and it also lacks a village shop. Non-campers will have to walk or acquire a lift into Moffat (unless sometime in the future accommodation again opens up in Beattock).

It is a listed building, so will not be demolished, but its future is unclear at the time of writing.

Lochhouse Tower

On the journey from Beattock into Moffat, Lochhouse Tower on the right of the road will be seen to good effect. It was originally built in the 1500s as a fortified tower offering protection in the troubled times of the Border Reivers, when there were constant disputes over the lands either side of the present Scottish/English border. There are several of these towers in the area and in the neighbouring Scottish Borders, two of which will later be passed on the SUW (see Stage 9). Most of the towers are in ruins today, as is the nearby Frenchland Tower on the east side of Moffat, but Lochhouse was restored in the 20th century and is now a private residence. There once stood such a tower at Corehead at the foot of the Devil's Beef Tub, but no traces of this remain today.

REST DAY – MOFFAT AND ENVIRONS

After a week of walking and having arrived in Moffat, the psychological if not exact halfway stage of the SUW, some walkers will want to have a rest day before continuing on the Way eastwards (or end the western half of the walk here, and return at a later date to complete it). A day (and more!) could easily be spent in and around the town, sight-seeing and enjoying the facilities on offer. Moffat is the most suitable place for a rest day on your itinerary. To move on without further exploration would mean that one of the best areas of the Southern Uplands has been neglected. The notes below should be useful in planning your day.

Moffat

Moffat has been in the tourist business for a long time, although it was initially the sheep industry that brought its wealth. The importance of hill farming to the local economy is evidenced by the Colvin Fountain in the High Street, which is one of Scotland's widest. The stone Moffat Ram sits atop the fountain, which was erected in 1875 and restored in 2004. Also of note in the High Street is the War Memorial, the Clock Tower and Moffat House, the latter built by John Adam and now a hotel.

A local girl, Rachel Whiteford, discovered Moffat Well in 1633, so turning the town into a fashionable spa, to which the wealthy and famous visited to 'take the waters'. A century later in 1748 Hartfell Spa was also discovered and the trickle of visitors became a flood. Spa water was piped into the town to the Baths House, a building that today serves as the Town Hall.

The small museum in the town details the history of Moffat and its surrounding countryside, tales of sheep

farming, cattle rustling, clan warfare, Covenanters, a mail
coach disaster and tourism. Among the occupants of the
churchyard lies the body of John McAdam, the famous
road builder. The most famous inn in the town is the
Black Bull, which dates from 1568. Claverhouse, the
persecutor of the Covenanters, lodged here in the 17th
century and Robert Burns scratched a poem on a
windowpane, a copy of which is kept in the bar.

Tourists today come mainly to visit the highly
successful Moffat Woollen Mill and the new
Hammerlands Centre, and of course to chew the famous
Moffat Toffee. Moffat has all the facilities that any visitor
could wish for, including accommodation of every type
and standard, from comfortable 2- and 3-star hotels to a
plentiful supply of B&B establishments. There is an excellent large campsite in the town operated by the Camping
and Caravan Club. An abundance of both gift shops and
cafés/restaurants and pubs serve the town.

Near to Moffat are two local beauty spots worthy of
mention that should not be missed by those with time
available:

The Devil's Beef Tub

This large depression beneath Annanhead Hill and
enclosed by Great Hill and Ericstane Hill is some five
miles north-north-west of Moffat at the head of
Annanwater. It is so named because at the time of the
Border Reivers, cattle thieves used to hide their stolen
stock here, and is mentioned by Sir Walter Scott in his
novel *Redgauntlet*. There are plenty of historical associations with this scenic area. William Wallace's
brother-in-law farmed at Corehead at the foot of the Tub.
Covenanters were chased and shot in the Beef Tub in the
17th century: a memorial to John Hunter above the Beef
Tub commemorates one such shooting. On the A701
above the Beef Tub, from where one of the best views of
the Tub are available, two mailmen died in a terrible
snow storm in 1831; their remains lie in Moffat churchyard and a memorial to them can be found on the
roadside near the Tub.

The Grey Mare's Tail

North of Moffat along Moffatdale, a classic example of a glaciated valley, lies one of the most well-known beauty spots in the south of Scotland, the Grey Mare's Tail waterfall, owned by the National Trust for Scotland. The waters of Loch Skeen, in a glacial hanging valley in the Moffat Hills high above the A708, plunge down around 60m (200ft) by a series of cascades into Moffat Water. A good footpath allows access to a superb viewpoint of the waterfall.

Hill Walks in the Moffat Hills

Those walkers who would like a day off from the SUW, but who are keen to sample the marvellous hill country in the neighbourhood, are strongly encouraged to consider a hill walk to the Devil's Beef Tub and/or Hart Fell, which lie a few miles to the north of the town, above the Upper Annandale (Annanwater) Valley. The walk along Annanwater is a very pleasant and easy one, but if coupled with an ascent of Hart Fell will make for a long day. A good solution for this would be to hire a taxi for the 4½ mile drive up the Annanwater valley to Annanwater Hall (GR NT 075103) or to the end of the public road at Ericstane, where the walks described below begin. Either arrange for a taxi to meet you at the end of your hill day, or else enjoy the stroll back to Moffat, taking the delightful riverside path (signposted at GR NT 079070) along the River Annan, reaching the town opposite the popular Station Park.

The walks outlined below are hill walks over fairly rough and uninhabited country. It cannot be emphasised too strongly that they should only be undertaken by experienced, fit and well-equipped hillwalkers. The skills and experience necessary to accomplish safely the hill walks below are considerably greater than those required to walk the waymarked SUW. There are few paths to be found on these fells, except for some grassy tracks that have been formed over the years by shepherds using quad bikes. There are no footpath signposts, other than the sign for the public path to

Hartfell Spa at GR NT 075104. No walker should attempt these routes without carrying the relevant map, either OS Landranger 78 or Explorer 330, a compass and **the ability to use them**. Hill fog is not uncommon in the Southern Uplands (as you are no doubt by now aware!) and those unfamiliar with this type of landscape can easily become disorientated in such conditions. Precise navigation is essential.

Hart Fell and the Devil's Beef Tub

Strong walkers are recommended the following hill walk, which will show the best that the Moffat Hills have to offer. From the end of the public road at Ericstane follow the single-track private road for about a mile to Corehead Farmhouse. Pass to the back of the farmhouse (white building) and cross a small stream to exit via a fieldgate into the lower reaches of the Devil's Beef Tub. Locate the path (marked on OS maps) that climbs and traverses the western flank of Great Hill (in icy/snowy/very wet conditions this path, which has some slight exposure, can be dangerous). On reaching the col to the west of the summit bear to the right (eastwards) to attain the top of Great Hill (466m; 1528ft small cairn). There are good views from this vantage point westwards to the Lowthers, south-westwards to Queensberry Hill, southwards down Upper Annandale and eastwards towards Hart Fell. There is a huge expanse of hill and moorland to the north, towards the Fruid, Talla and Megget Reservoirs. Follow the superb ridge eastwards over Chalk Rig Edge (499m; 1637ft) and Spout Craig (562m; 1843ft) to Whitehope Heights and Whitehope Knowe (614m; 2014ft). There is a short descent here before the long, steep climb up to the summit trig point of Hart Fell (808m; 2650ft), a Corbett and the highest point in the Moffat Hills, an expansive viewpoint. Make the descent over Arthur's Seat (731m; 2398ft) and down the long south-western ridge of the mountain back to Annanwater and so to Moffat.

Two other first-rate options involve traverses of the Moffat hills.

Corehead House by the Devil's Beef Tub

Black Hope Valley and Hart Fell

The Black Hope Valley is one of the best examples of a glaciated mountain valley in the Southern Uplands. The view of the U-shaped valley and meandering Blackhope Burn from the upper reaches of Black Hope is quite outstanding. Take a taxi from Moffat for approximately 5½ miles along the A708 Selkirk Road up the Moffat Water Valley to the farm of Cappelgill. Leave the road at Black Hope Cottage and follow the track up the Black Hope Valley. Where it ends continue upwards on ever steepening ground, crossing Whirley Gill and following the line of Cold Grain to emerge at the summit trig of Hart Fell. Follow the ridge westwards over Whitehope Knowe and Heights and descend to Upper Annandale either from the col to the west of Spout Craig or on the Beef Tub Path down the western flank of Great Hill. Return to Moffat on foot on the Annanwater Road (or arrange for a taxi to meet you at the beginning of the public road at Ericstane).

It was here in 1990 that a long bow dating from 4000BC (several centuries before the famous Ice Man of the Austrian/Italian Alps was found by a passing hill walker.

The Traverse of the Moffat Hills from the Grey Mare's Tail to the Devil's Beef Tub

To commence this classic traverse of the Moffat Hills take a taxi along the A708 Selkirk Road, up the Moffat Water Valley to the National Trust for Scotland's car park at the Grey Mare's Tail Waterfall, a journey of about 10 miles. After viewing the waterfall from the path to the west of the Tail Burn, return to the car park to start the traverse by taking the path to the east of the Tail Burn to climb up to Lock Skeen. From here climb Loch Craig Head (800m; 2624ft) and then in a southerly direction for a couple of kilometres over Donald's Cleuch Head and Firthope Rig (801m; 2627ft) before bearing south-westwards over Rotten Bottom at the head of the Garrifran Valley. ◀ The Garrifran Valley is undergoing ecological restoration at present, whereby deer and sheep are excluded so that eventually the landscape will revert to its former natural state. The summit of Hart Fell is reached via Hartfell Rig, and from here the traverse is completed via the Whitehopes, Craig Spout, Chalk Rig Edge, Great Hill and Annanhead Hill (478m; 1568ft). The latter hill is crowned by a trig point which bears the number of '5678'. Descend the southern ridge of the hill to the small car park at GR NT 056128. A taxi could be arranged to meet walkers here, as this is quite a long day for most people (although do visit the Covenanter's Monument and Orientation Table before leaving for Moffat – see below).

Great Hill above Annanwater in the Moffat Hills

120

However, very strong walkers can return to Moffat on foot. First visit the memorial to the two mail coach employees who died in the Great Snow Storm of February 1831. This is at GR NT 052129 on the side of the A701. ▶ Return from the memorial to visit the Covenanter's Monument and Orientation Table at GR NT 061126. ▶ Continue south along the A701 (or better traverse over Ericstane Hill) to leave the road at GR NT 060115. Follow the track marked on the map (this is the Old Edinburgh Road which was in use before the new A701 was built in 1829 and was the route used by the ill-fated mail coach in 1831). Follow this often wet and muddy track down to Meikleholmside and then the Annanwater Road (and riverside path if preferred) back to Moffat. It is stressed that this complete walk, from the Grey Mare's Tail to Moffat is only for very fit and prepared walkers.

Take care, as some drivers can be quite reckless along this rather dangerous road.

From here there is a superb view down into the Beef Tub and over to the Hart Fell Range.

Walking options for shorter, easier days include the following:

1. Corehead > Beef Tub path (as described above) > col to the west of Great Hill > west to summit trig of Annanhill Hill > descend west to the A701 (the monument to the mail coach victims of 1831 is situated about 400m to the left along this road) > right along the A701 (care) to visit the Covenanter's Monument and Orientation Table at GR NT 061126 > continue south on road (or alternatively over Ericstane Hill) to GR NT 060115 > take the track marked on the OS maps (the Old Edinburgh Road) southwards to Meikleholmside and the Annanwater Valley > south back to Moffat, taking the riverside path starting at GR NT 079070.

2. Corehead > Devil's Beef Tub > Great Hill > Chalk Rig Edge > col between Chalk Rig Edge and Spout Craig > descend southwards from here back to Upper Annandale.

3. Annanwater Hall (GR NT 075103) > public footpath to Hartfell Spa. Return by the same route.

STAGE 8

Beattock (Moffat) to Tibbie Shiels (St Mary's Loch)

20.9 miles (33.6km) + 1.3 miles (2.1km)

| | Distance (miles) | | Distance (km) | |
	Sectional	Cumulative	Sectional	Cumulative
Moffat	0	119.0*	0	191.5*
Beattock	(1.3)	119.0*	(2.1)	191.5*
Craigbeck Hope+	4.9	123.9	7.9	199.4
Ettrick Head	3.3	127.2	5.3	204.7
Over Phawhope Bothy	1.7	128.9	2.7	207.4
Potburn	0.4	129.3	0.7	208.1
Scabcleuch	5.7	135.0	9.1	217.2
Riskinhope Hope	2.8	137.8	4.5	221.7
Tibbie Shiels	2.1	139.9	3.4	225.1

* Moffat is a 1.3 mile (2.1km) detour from the SUW. This distance is not added to the cumulative distance along the SUW.
+ On original route only

Summary
If you are beginning by now to feel the effects of too many hard, over-long days then take heart, as the walk over to St Mary's Loch is the last of the really long stages on the SUW. Today the walker enters the Scottish Borders and from then on more towns and villages will be encountered than in the more remote and sparsely populated Dumfries & Galloway Region, and hence there will be more possibilities for obtaining accommodation and other facilities, and shorter daily stages are feasible. Those wanting to shorten today's stage, to give two more equal days between Moffat and Traquair, should arrange a vehicle pick-up from the Ettrick valley,

preferably at Scabcleuch, thus making this stage 25.7km (16 miles) from Beattock, and tomorrow's stage 27.2km (16.9 miles) to Traquair.

The SUW skirts the south of Moffat over three major rivers, Evan Water, the River Annan and finally Moffat Water. Just before descending to Moffat Water the Way passes over a steep little hill with offers good views of Moffat, Gallow Hill and the Annanwater valley. A delightful deciduous wood, the most attractive encountered on the SUW, is traversed before the route finally pulls away from Moffat to head into the Ettrick Hills.

The SUW through the area of forestry to the east of Moffat Water, south-west of Gateshaw Rig, has been prone to frequent temporary diversions over the years to avoid forestry operations. To avoid both these problems and a long trudge through forestry plantations, the Rangers have now (summer 2007) opened up and waymarked a new high level route of the SUW in this region. It leaves the original route of the SUW at grid reference NT122043 and rejoins at grid reference NT160058, a distance of about 5½ km, after a high level ridge walk over Gateshaw Rig and Croft Head followed by a steep descent of Cat Shoulder. This new trail is to become the standard route of the SUW, but the original route via Craigbeck Hope will remain as a lower level, easier alternative, but subject to temporary closure during forestry operations. The new route is scenically far superior to the original trail, with good views back to Moffat on the ascent to Gateshaw Rig and excellent views over to the Hart Fell and White Coomb ranges from Croft Head. However, this adds additional effort to an already long stage. About 180m of steep extra ascent and descent is required, although the length of the new trail is similar to that of the original route. It crosses the 600m contour line on Croft Head, and in adverse weather conditions the prudent may wish to opt for the original, low level route through the forestry plantations.

After the two routes rejoin there follows a superb section of open hillside up to Ettrick Head, offering great views of the Ettrick Hills. The route crosses the boundary fence from Dumfries & Galloway into the Scottish Borders. Shelter and a rest (maybe lunch) is possible in Over Phawhope Bothy, before tackling the several miles of easy walking along the scenic and remote Ettrick Valley. The section ends with one of the classic hill routes in southern Scotland, over to St Mary's Loch in the Yarrow Valley. Here will be found one of the most famous hostelries in Scotland, the old Tibbie Shiels Inn on St Mary's Loch, which offers bed and breakfast accommodation and allows camping in its adjacent field.

Route

On leaving your accommodation in Moffat there are two possibilities for continuing the SUW. Either retrace your steps back to the Old Brig Inn and roundabout in Beattock to resume exactly where you left off, or else cut a few kilometres off the SUW by taking the minor road from Moffat towards Wamphray. There is little merit in following the actual line of the SUW south around Moffat, so the latter is the recommended option of choice. It will be described first, before the full route of the SUW.

For the 'short-cut' route to the SUW

From the War Memorial in the centre of Moffat, head along the Selkirk Road, the A708. Pass the entrance drive to Hammerlands Garden Centre and the Rugby Club on the right and soon afterwards take the minor road (Old Carlisle Road) signposted to Wamphray. Follow this out of town for about 2km to cross the bridge over Moffat Water. This is the point where the SUW is picked up (see below).

To resume the SUW in Beattock

Return to the roundabout in Beattock where the SUW was left. Opposite the Old Brig Inn (now closed) turn right onto a track enclosed by an avenue of trees. At its end, bear left to reach the river (Evan Water) and pass under the M74 motorway. Follow the metalled lane eastwards under high-tension cables, the fourth line of valley communication (after the railway, A74 and M74).

Map continues p. 128

The lane eventually crosses a bridge over the River Annan to reach a

T-junction. Cross a stile opposite to climb the steep grassy hill ahead. From the high point of the climb, at around 140m (460ft), there is a grand view to the north of the town of Moffat below the wooded Gallow Hill. Cross a stile where fence and old dry stone wall (dyke) meet, continuing over the hill to a stile on its other side, and descend alongside a wall to a ladder stile, which leads onto a narrow sylvan lane. Turn left here walking upstream along **Moffat Water.** Turn right at a T-junction to cross the river. This is the point at which the 'short-cut' route from Moffat along the Wamphray Road joins the SUW.

The SUW continued

About 50m after the bridge turn left over a short ladder stile, just before another lane on the left. A notice at this point warns 'Persons pass through the wood at their own risk'! Most people would consider a walk through this marvellous old, deciduous woodland to be well worth the (negligible) risk. This woodland, Dumcrieff, is the finest beech wood in Annandale and is such a refreshing contrast from the many sterile, dark, forbidding sitka spruce plantations that unfortunately blight too much of the wonderful landscape of southern Scotland. Many rhododendrons line the path and these offer a blaze of colour during May and June. Holly, at its best at Christmas time, is also abundant in this woodland. Emerging from the wood, walk in a field dotted with more attractive trees, alongside Moffat Water. Exit the field onto a road to the right of an arched bridge over Moffat Water. Do not cross back over the river but cross the road to walk ahead on a gravel track (left on the road leads in about 350m to the A708 from where it is about 2.5km back into Moffat – this route into town is not recommended for pedestrians as the road is a main one, having several dangerous bends).

The track follows Moffat Water for a few hundred metres before climbing the hillside to the right, to reach the edge of forestry at a cattle grid and gate, grid reference NT122043. This is the point where the two routes diverge.

High Level route (opened summer 2007)

Cross the cattle grid, turn left to descend for 30m to cross a footbridge over the Cornal Burn. Climb through the trees, bearing left to reach and follow a dry stone wall uphill. The path eventually veers to the right to leave the wall and crosses Littlehope Burn. Continue on the path to reach a forest road where you bear right. On reaching the edge of forestry the trail bears left to climb steeply uphill to the right of Dry Gutter to meet a forest track (those wishing to rejoin the original route of the SUW can do so here by turning right to descend on this track). Turn left on the track and follow it for about 700m to a point where the track bears sharply to the left. Leave the track at this point to climb the wooden steps ahead to leave the plantation and gain access to Gateshaw Rig (567m). Pass over this top, now following the line of a fence along the ridge, first to the north-east and finally northwards to commence the descent down Cat Shoulder, following the fence line at first before taking a series of path zig-zags down to the circular stone sheepfold at grid reference NT160058, where the original route of the SUW is rejoined.

Original Route

Note that if temporary diversion signs are in evidence, as a result of forestry operations, then please be sure to follow them. Cross the cattle grid, remaining on the wide forest track, following Cornal Burn down to your left, until a track 'Y' junction is encountered: bear left here to continue on the track past **Craigbeck Hope**, noting the interesting ornamental stone lions guarding the entrance to this house. Soon after this drive ignore a track off to the left, but continue ahead now contouring the hillside to the south of Gateshaw Rig.

The track eventually descends down to the right, skirting Birch Hill to the west of the 688m (2257ft) Loch Fell. At a tight hairpin bend in this track, at an attractive stone marker post indicating 8½ miles to Eskdalemuir, leave the track by taking a footpath on the left, heading north through a forest ride. There should be SUW Leaflet

Boxes here. These will be the last such free leaflets that SUW walkers will encounter, for soon you will pass the boundary from Dumfries & Galloway into the Scottish Borders, and it is not the policy of the Borders Region to provide such leaflets.

The path climbs alongside a babbling burn in a very steep-sided upper valley beneath the 636m (2086ft) high Croft Head, and enters some superb open country. Shapely **Capel Fell** (678m; 2224ft) soon comes into view, with the distinctive Craigmichan Scar on its flanks. On reaching a circular stone sheep fold, at the foot of Cat Shoulder, the new route

Map continues p. 130

joins this original route. The SUW climbs to the right (south-east) of the Scar above a very deeply cut mountain valley and offers views down the cleft of the Selcoth Glen to the north-west. The

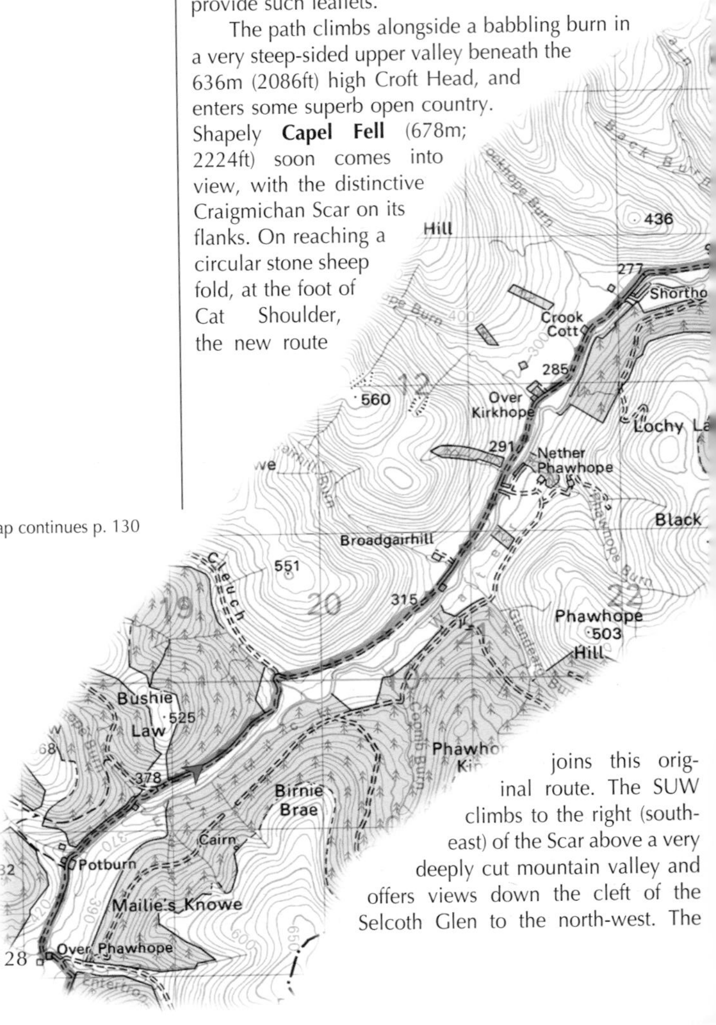

Map labels: Back Burn, ockhope Burn, Hill, ·436, ·277, Shortho, Crook Cott, ·285, ·560, Over Kirkhope, ·291, Nether Phawhope, Lochy La, Black, Broadgairhill, ·551, ·315, Phawhope, ·503, Hill, Phawho Ki, Bushie Law, ·525, ·378, Birnie Brae, Cairn, Potburn, Mailie's Knowe, Over Phawhope

430'

410'

Scabcleuch Burn

487
Craig Hill
Cairns

435
Scabcleuch
Hill
Scabcleuch

253

Ettrick Ho

ssarshill

erig

Gra

traversing path has a steep drop to the left for a while, where care is required, particularly in icy conditions or where snow covers the hill.

Cross a bridge over a mountain stream, pass a 'stone man' sculpture and climb the steep bank above. The path soon reaches the boundary fence between Dumfries & Galloway and the Scottish Borders, where a sign welcomes you to the Scottish Borders. After around 127 miles (205km) on a complete west to east traverse of Dumfries & Galloway, you finally say goodbye to the region and begin your long journey of some 85 miles (136km) through the Borders to the east coast of Scotland. The path begins its descent and alas, after the excellent section of open hillside over **Ettrick Head**, the route now soon re-enters the trees of a forestry plantation. The Way reaches a forest track at a bend in the latter: turn right along this track and in about 2km you will reach the bothy of **Over Phawhope** (see Appendix 1). This is a most pleasant bothy with a pleasing view from the window, in front of which should be found a table and chairs. A wood burning stove provides heating, fuel for which is often left by the Ranger (although do not rely on this). A picnic table should be found outside the bothy, but beware of the midges in season! A Southern Upland Way Information Board is nearby.

On leaving the bothy cross the stream by the footbridge and follow the track to **Potburn**. Pass the rather neglected buildings of Potburn, to continue north-eastwards along the valley. Less than a kilometre after Potburn the track becomes metalled, at a signpost indicating the trail to 'Bodesbeck Law and the Ettrick Horseshoe'. Ignore this and stay on this quiet, narrow road heading down the Ettrick Valley for a little over 9km after Potburn. Ettrick Water is a constant companion, meandering along the valley floor down to your right on this long road section, which offers easy walking with good valley and hill views. Continue down the Ettrick Valley all the way to Scabcleuch Farm. If time and energy are still available a visit to Ettrick Kirk is recommended (see Places of Interest). To reach the church simply continue ahead along the Ettrick Valley for a further 1.3km. Return by the same route to **Scabcleuch** to continue along the SUW.

The SUW leaves the Ettrick Valley at Scabcleuch to take to the hills to the north along the public footpath that links the Ettrick Valley with the Yarrow Valley and St Mary's Loch. The footpath climbs at first beside Scabcleuch Burn, between the very steep slopes of Craig Hill on the east and the gentler inclines of Scabcleuch Hill on the west. You are following one of the classic hill tracks in the Borders. It climbs to skirt Peniestone Knowe before descending to **Riskinhope**. On the way pass and ignore a signpost indicating another right of way to Ettrick Church (this is a very rough route). Continue ahead for Riskinhope. On Pikestone Rig be sure to take the right-hand path at a fork (the left-hand path descends to the Loch of the Lowes).

Descend to cross Crosscleuch Burn by way of a wooden footbridge and then climb to skirt the south and east sides of Earl's Hill to reach a SUW fingerpost, which also indicates another trail off to the right, to Hopehouse via the Captain's Road. Keep ahead on the SUW to reach a track at the edge of forestry. Turn left on this pleasant grassy track to descend towards St Mary's Loch. If conditions are clear it will be possible to make out in the valley below the white statue of James Hogg, the Ettrick Shepherd, on the left below the wood at the foot of Ox Cleuch. It is worth a short detour on reaching **Tibbie Shiels** to visit this famous monument to this area's most celebrated poet. You will finally descend to the point between the two lochs of St Mary's and of the Lowes. Turn right for the famous Tibbie Shiels Inn and your night's accommodation. Yet another Southern Upland Way Information board stands here.

Loch of the Lowes and St Mary's Loch seen from the slopes of East Muchra Hill

131

James Hogg statue,
Tibbie Shiels

PLACES OF INTEREST

The Ettrick Hills

A large range of sparsely populated and infrequently visited hills on the southern edge of the central Southern Uplands, bounded by Annandale, Moffatdale, the Yarrow Valley and Ettrick Forest. The major summits form a horseshoe around the isolated Ettrick Valley: Herman Law (614m; 2014ft), Andrewhinney Hill (677m; 2221ft), Bell Craig (624m; 2047ft), Bodesbeck Law (662m; 2171ft), Capel Fell (678m; 2224ft), Croft Head (637m; 2089ft), Loch Fell (688m; 2257ft), Wind Fell (665m; 2181ft) and Ettrick Pen (692m; 2270ft).

Craigmichan Scar

One of the most dramatic stretches of the SUW is that up to Ettrick Head high above Moffatdale. The underlying rocks of the gently rounded grassy hills of the Southern Uplands are sometimes exposed, particularly on very steep ground, and are so here on the southern side of Capel Fell in a savage ravine above Selcoth Burn. Bare rock and scree abound and erosion is becoming more of a problem as the years pass.

Ettrick Kirk

This lonely, isolated church is situated 1.3km off the route of the SUW (from Scabcleuch), but is easily

James Hogg tombstone, Ettrick Kirkyard

reached on a quiet minor road and if time and energy are available a visit is recommended to experience its tranquil simplicity. It still serves the scattered rural communities along the remote Ettrick Valley. The churchyard holds the remains of both James Hogg, the Ettrick Shepherd, and Tibbie Shiels (see below and under 'Places of Interest' in Stage 9) whose bodies were carried over the hills to be buried here, on the old 'corpse road' from the Yarrow Valley. Another 200m further east along the Ettrick Valley road will be found the James Hogg Memorial, built at the site of his birthplace.

Tibbie Shiels
Tibbie Shiels and her husband, a mole-catcher by trade, lived here in a small cottage by the shore of St Mary's Loch in the 19th century. But the husband died at a very early age leaving Tibbie to cope and bring up her six children alone. She converted the cottage into an inn, serving travellers on this wild, high road between Moffat and Selkirk in the Borders. She gained quite a reputation as a hard, independent, strong but much revered and loved character. She also entertained in her lonely wayside inn such notables as Sir Walter Scott and James Hogg, the Ettrick Shepherd. This remarkable woman died in around 1878 at the age of 95.

Today the Tibbie Shiels Inn remains one of Scotland's most famous hostelries and SUW walkers should consider it a privilege to spend the night there. An ancient photograph of Tibbie usually hangs on the wall in the bar. On the wall of the Tibbie Shiels Inn there is a plaque commemorating the opening of the SUW on this spot on 27th April, 1984 by Michael Ancram, the then Minister for Home Affairs and the Environment at the Scottish Office.

STAGE 9

Tibbie Shiels (St Mary's Loch) to Traquair (Innerleithen)

12.0 miles (19.3km) + 1.3 miles (2.1km)

| | Distance (miles) | | Distance (km) | |
	Sectional	Cumulative	Sectional	Cumulative
Tibbie Shiels	0	139.9	0	225.1
North-east end of				
St Mary's Loch (A 708)	3.3	143.2	5.3	230.4
Blackhouse	2.4	145.6	3.9	234.3
Blake Muir (461m)	2.9	148.5	4.6	238.9
Traquair	3.4	151.9*	5.5	244.4*
Innerleithen	(1.3)	151.9*	(2.1)	244.4*

* Innerleithen is a 1.3 mile (2.1km) detour from the SUW. This distance is not added to the cumulative distance along the SUW.

Summary

A short stage will no doubt be welcomed after the exertions of yesterday. If an early start is made it should be possible to reach Traquair for lunch, even if a slightly late one. This will provide time to visit historic Traquair House, one of southern Scotland's great country houses. Lunch can be taken in the excellent tearoom at Traquair House, after which allow at least a couple of hours to do justice to the house, brew house and gardens. The house and grounds are open daily from the end of March to the end of October, varying times, and at weekends during November (admission charge).

The stage starts with a 5km walk along the shore of southern Scotland's largest inland loch, St Mary's Loch, a bracing walk, particularly if a strong breeze is up, which hopefully will be a sou'westerly and so behind you.

On the SUW descending towards Traquair

A fine cross-country route follows, from St Mary's Loch to Traquair, with good ridge walking on some pleasant footpaths. The ruins of two ancient fortified towers, at Dryhope and at Blackhouse, are passed, reminders of a more troubled time in these parts. A few centuries after the era of the Border Reivers, tracks in the Borders were developed into drove roads to transport livestock south to the English markets. The area between St Mary's Loch, Traquair, Selkirk and Galashiels is criss-crossed with such old drove roads and more of these will be used before the SUW is completed.

There is the option of spending the night in Traquair village at the end of the stage or in the neighbouring small town of Innerleithen.

Route
The next 5km of the SUW follows the eastern shore of St Mary's Loch. Leaving **Tibbie Shiels**, pass in front of St Mary's Loch Sailing Club premises, and start out on the footpath that follows the shore of the loch, with the water on your

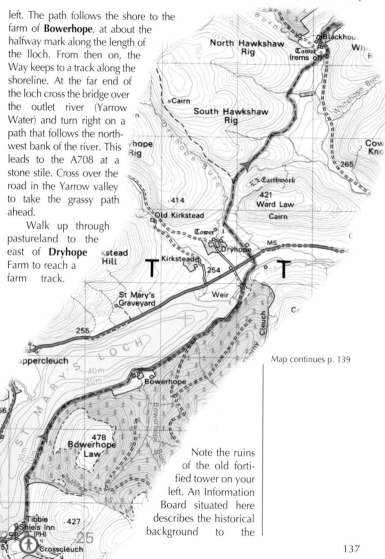

left. The path follows the shore to the farm of **Bowerhope**, at about the halfway mark along the length of the lloch. From then on, the Way keeps to a track along the shoreline. At the far end of the loch cross the bridge over the outlet river (Yarrow Water) and turn right on a path that follows the north-west bank of the river. This leads to the A708 at a stone stile. Cross over the road in the Yarrow valley to take the grassy path ahead.

Walk up through pastureland to the east of **Dryhope** Farm to reach a farm track.

Map continues p. 139

Note the ruins of the old forti-fied tower on your left. An Information Board situated here describes the historical background to the

137

St Mary's Loch seen from the SUW

tower. Turn right onto the track and follow it northwards to the west of the hill of Ward Law (420m; 1378ft). Leave the track for a path on the right after about 400m, the path heading north-east towards **Blackhouse Tower** and Farm. It climbs over the shoulder of South Hawkshaw Rig and then drops down towards Douglas Burn (note the ravine of Whitehope Burn over to the right). Drop down to cross a stream in a wooded dip by a long wooden footbridge and steps. The SUW descends towards Blackhouse and crosses the right-hand of two wooden footbridges over Douglas Burn (i.e. with Blackhouse on your left, not as the route is shown on some old maps). Bear left on the track towards Blackhouse and note the ruins of another ancient tower house here. Pass to the right of the farm buildings and tower, but immediately, in front of a gate leading to a barn, turn right onto a grassy path. So begins another long ascent on the SUW.

The path soon enters a plantation as it climbs to the east of Craighope Burn. Just before the top of the climb be sure to look back for your last glimpse of St Mary's Loch and the Moffat and Ettrick Hills. The trail emerges onto open moorland to the east of Deuchar Law (542m; 1778ft) with fine views of the distant Moorfoot Hills ahead. The SUW fortunately does not touch this range, which presents some of the toughest terrain underfoot in all the Southern Uplands. But for SUW walkers, springy turf and splendid ridges follow for a couple of miles as the trail passes over **Blake Muir** (461m; 1512ft).

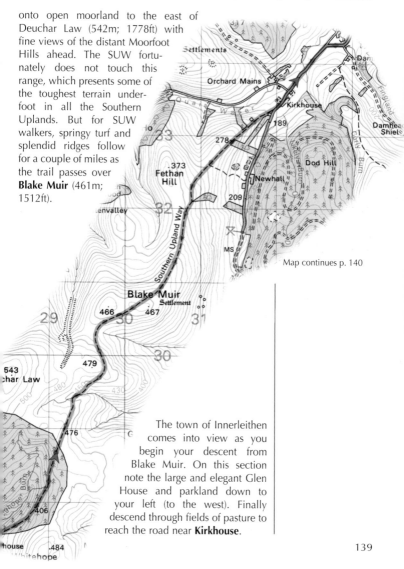

Map continues p. 140

The town of Innerleithen comes into view as you begin your descent from Blake Muir. On this section note the large and elegant Glen House and parkland down to your left (to the west). Finally descend through fields of pasture to reach the road near **Kirkhouse**.

139

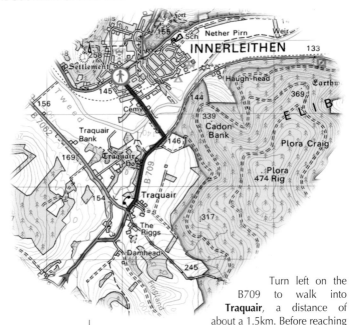

Turn left on the B709 to walk into **Traquair**, a distance of about a 1.5km. Before reaching the village, note but ignore the footpath signpost at Damhead indicating a route 'to the Yarrow Valley via Glengaber (8 ml)'. Arrive eventually at the crossroads in Traquair by the War Memorial (public telephone here). If continuing along the SUW then turn right, but if stopping in Traquair there are a couple of B&B establishments in the village, and a visit to historic Traquair House is a 'must do' whilst in the area. For Traquair House turn left at the crossroads at the War Memorial to follow the B7062 for about 700m before turning right on the drive to the House. More choice of B&B and also hotel accommodation is available in larger Innerleithen, where there is also a campsite, the latter located beside the River Tweed. To reach **Innerleithen** continue along the B709 for just over two extra kilometres to cross the River Tweed and enter the town.

PLACES OF INTEREST

St Mary's Loch and the Loch of the Lowes

St Mary's Loch, shaped rather like a banana, is about 5km long and more than 40m deep, the largest natural loch in the Borders and Lothian Region. Before the last Ice Age there was just one 6.5km long loch, but now a delta separates the Loch of the Lowes to the south from the larger St Mary's Loch. This has resulted from deposits that have been washed down from the hills, over the millennia, by the Crosscleuch and Ox Cleuch Burns, a process that is still continuing today. Within another ten millennia there will be three lochs here, alluvial deposits from Megget Water producing another delta so cutting St Mary's Loch into two stretches of water. Both of the present day lochs derive their names from the Church of St Mary of the Lowes, first recorded in 1292.

The best view of St Mary's Loch and the Loch of the Lowes is, in the author's opinion, off-route of the SUW, in that the lochs are best seen from the northern slopes of East Muchra Hill, a little way below the summit in afternoon sunlight. The Loch of the Lowes and the

St Mary's Loch from the upper reaches of Ox Cleuch

southern arm of St Mary's Loch then stretch way below the observer, cradled in the steep-sided surrounding hills, Hogg's *'dappled vales of heaven'*. Another good viewpoint of the two lochs is from the slopes of Ox Cleuch on the west side of the A708. Whilst admiring these stunning views do contemplate Hogg's verse, which demonstrates so well his love of this region:

> Oft had he viewed, as morning rose,
> The bosom of the lonely Lowes:
> Oft thrilled his heart at close of even
> To see the dappled vales of heaven,
> With many a mountain, moor and tree,
> Asleep upon St Mary.
> *James Hogg, the Ettrick Shepherd (1770–1835)*

After Robert Burns, James Hogg is the most revered poet in southern Scotland. Hogg was the epitome of the self-educated man, being forced to leave school at the age of seven, but whilst employed as a lowly herdsman in the Yarrow valley he taught himself to read and write, such that by the age of thirty he was fully conversant with the greatest writers of the English language. He married one Margaret Philips and enjoyed life as both a hill farmer and as a poet and writer. He made occasional visits to Edinburgh where he was celebrated by the most notable writers of the day, but never deserted his life and home in the Borders, generally shunning urban sophistication; he *'Held worldly pomp in high derision'*. On his death in 1835, his funeral in Ettrick Kirk was attended by a huge gathering of both locals, including Tibbie Shiels, and literary figures from Edinburgh and beyond. These notables must have appeared most out of place on the muddy tracks of 19th-century Scotland, on the coffin route over from the Yarrow valley to Ettrick Kirk.

James Hogg Monument

A most impressive statue of James Hogg seated on a large plinth will be found on the A708 opposite the track leading to Tibbie Shiels Inn. Examples of some of his verse are inscribed on the sides and rear of the plinth.

The nearby 'Info Centre' near Hogg's statue is somewhat hidden behind a small dry stone wall windbreak, but should not be missed. Three interpretative boards will be found there offering much information on sheep farming in the area, the changing nature of the two lochs over the past 10,000 years and in the future, and finally on the life and poetry of James Hogg.

A hundred metres or so from the Monument is the pleasant fair trade Glen Café and Bistro, an alternative to Tibbie Shiels if desired. Food is served here all day and also during the evenings on summer weekends, and comfy armchairs and free newspapers are on offer, very enticing at the end of a hard day's walk. The Bistro offers a number of special dinner concerts throughout the year, offering mainly folk music and poetry, particularly that of James Hogg.

Gordon Arms Hotel

Another famous hostelry of the Borders, this establishment is off-route, lying 3.5km east of the point where the SUW leaves the A708 at the north-east end of St Mary's Loch. It is notable for being the place where Sir Walter Scott and James Hogg met for the very last time in the autumn of 1830. Scott was to die first in 1832, Hogg following him just three years later.

Dryhope

Dryhope Tower, now in ruins, was built in the 14th century for defensive purposes at the time of the Border Reivers. An information board alongside the SUW gives more detail about the tower.

Blackhouse

James Hogg, the Ettrick Shepherd, was herdsman here in his younger days, from 1790 to 1800. The ruins of yet another fortified tower lie at the back of the present day farm.

Blackhouse

Traquair House

Marketed as the oldest continuously inhabited house in Scotland, Traquair had very humble beginnings going back as far as AD950, with its 'modern wings' being completed in 1680. The Stuarts of Traquair had an unfortunate history in that they backed the wrong side in politics and religion, being ardent Catholics and strong supporters of the Jacobite cause. The first Laird died at Flodden Field in 1513 and later Earls were imprisoned and persecuted for their beliefs and political leanings.

The House is steeped in history. The famous Bear Gates stand at the original entrance drive but remain locked. ◀ Mary Queen of Scots spent some time here, when she was nursing the infant who was to become James VI of Scotland and I of England: his cradle is on display in the House. There are secret passages and priest holes to see, where illicit Catholic mass was said in those earlier troubled times. The old library is one of the finest rooms in the House. Outside there is a maze. Finally a trip to Traquair wouldn't be complete without a visit to Traquair House Brewery, dating from the 18th century and revived by the late Laird, Peter Maxwell Stuart, in 1965. It has the distinction of being the only British brewery to ferment entirely in oak.

The gates have been locked since 1745 when the fifth Earl of Traquair bade farewell to Bonnie Prince Charlie with the promise that the gates would not be opened until the Stuarts were returned to power.

Innerleithen

Two places of interest are worth a visit in the Victorian town of Innerleithen. In the High Street will be found Robert Smail's Printing Works, a most fascinating place to visit, in the care of the National Trust for Scotland. The printing works were set up in 1848 and remained in the Smail family until their closure in 1985. To visit there is to take a step back in time, as the works were never modernised and all is as it was in its heyday in the 19th century. The original machines are still in working order. Some distance out of the main town will be found St Ronan's Well. Innerleithen was a popular spa town visited by Burns and made famous by Sir Walter Scott in his book *St Ronan's Well*. There is hotel, B&B and campsite accommodation in Innerleithen, as well as grocery shops, pubs, cafés and restaurants.

Innerleithen seen on the approach to Traquair

STAGE 10

Traquair (Innerleithen) to Melrose

17.3 miles (27.8km) + 1.3 miles (2.1km)

	Distance (miles)		Distance (km)	
	Sectional	Cumulative	Sectional	Cumulative
Innerleithen	0	151.9*	0	244.4*
Traquair	(1.3)	151.9*	(2.1)	244.4*
Minch Moor (point 512m)	2.5	154.4	4.0	248.4
Brown Knowe (524m)	1.9	156.3	3.1	251.5
Three Brethren (464m)	3.2	159.5	5.1	256.6
Yair Bridge (River Tweed)	2.3	161.8	3.7	260.3
Galashiels	3.9	165.7	6.3	266.6
Melrose	3.5	169.2	5.6	272.2

* Innerleithen is a 1.3 mile (2.1km) detour from the SUW. This distance is not added to the cumulative distance along the SUW.

Summary
A stage with a great deal of variety, from splendid high level ridge walking, to the shores of the mellow River Tweed, from urban Galashiels to Melrose one of Scotland's most ancient and elegant towns complete with picturesque abbey ruins. From Traquair the Way follows one of the classic drove roads across the Border Hills. The route starts with a long climb first through woodland and then out onto open Minch Moor (or Minchmoor). This marks the last of the large forestry plantations on the SUW, as no more of any great dimensions are encountered on the route heading east from here. The SUW doesn't visit the actual summit of the moor, but a short optional diversion from the Way is all that is required to reach this fine viewpoint. A grand panoramic walk follows along a 6km ridge of open hillside, culminating in an ascent to the Three Brethren, one of the major stopping places on the local annual Ridings and a marvellous viewpoint.

The Three Brethren

From this highpoint the Way descends to the Tweed Valley at Yair, crossing the river by one of its finest stone-arched bridges. A climb over Hog Hill follows for a view down to Galashiels, a moderately large town where there is plentiful accommodation available for the night, for those wishing to break their journey here.

The stage continues with some semi-urban walking around Galashiels, but it soon leaves the town to skirt around Gala Hill from where there are superb views of the volcanic Eildon Hills and surrounding countryside. A section along the Gala Water and a disused railway line leads to a walk along the River Tweed into Melrose, with its picturesque ruined abbey, National Trust for Scotland Gardens and an abundance of teashops and restaurants, pubs and accommodation.

Route

If staying in Innerleithen overnight return to the War Memorial at the crossroads in the centre of **Traquair**. From here take the minor lane heading south-eastwards. This soon becomes a dirt track, so beginning the long ascent onto Minch Moor. A good grassy track climbs above the valley and passes to the left of the small Minch Moor Bothy. This is the most basic of the SUW bothies and the last one to be encountered. The need for bothy accommodation is now much less as the Way crosses the relatively more populated area of the Borders; the remote Galloway country is now far behind you. The SUW climbs steeply onto the Moor. It has been co-incident with a 'Tweeds Trail' route from Traquair, but on crossing a forest track be sure to take the right-hand of two paths (the left-hand one is a 'Tweeds Trail' route only). The trail climbs over **Pipers Knowe** and then over the northern flank of Minch Moor.

To reach the actual summit of **Minch Moor**, a recommended diversion in clear conditions, involves a short detour from the SUW of about 500m with about 55m of ascent. Before reaching the point at which the path to the summit leaves the SUW you should pass the 'Point of Resolution'. This is a conservation project and a 'sculpture', a series of ovals cut in the heather. It was completed in May 2005, as a pilot project intended to promote the idea of 'growing sculptures' along the length of the SUW, a 'Landworks' project. The 'Point of Resolution' sculpture is located at map reference NT 354337. It is quite likely that by the time you walk the SUW there will be other such sculptures for you to see along the Way.

There are good views on this ascent of the Moorfoot Hills to the north and down to the village of Walkerburn in the Tweed Valley. At the highest point on the SUW trail (point 512m; 1679ft) there is a footpath fingerpost which indicates the path to the right to the viewpoint and summit of Minch Moor (570m; 1870ft). ▶

The view from the summit, where there is a triangulation station, is extensive, well rewarding the extra effort.

From Point 512m continue ahead, now descending amongst trees. Walk downhill to cross over a forestry track, keeping on a footpath beside a plantation. This old Drove Road emerges from the trees as it climbs over **Hare Law** (509m; 1670ft). There now follows some 5.6km of glorious open moorland and hills, on a splendid ridge high above the Tweed Valley. The trail does not drop below the 450m contour line until it commences its final

Map continues p. 152

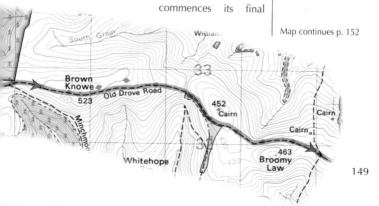

Minch Moor Bothy

descent to Yair after the Three Brethren. At the foot of Brown Knowe (523m; 1716ft) ignore the footpath on the right, the Minch Moor Road to Yarrowford (a 'Tweed Trail') but climb over the hill ahead. From the summit of **Browne Knowe** the triplet of the Eildon Hills above Melrose immediately catch the eye to the east. These three hills will be in view from high ground for very many more miles along the SUW.

Continue east along the Drove Road, now heading for point 451. After this spot height, the SUW skirts to the north of **Broomy Law** (463m; 1519ft), with wonderful rural views out to the left (north). A path ascends to Broomy Law's summit for those who cannot resist visiting every hill along the ridge. Shortly after this hill a ladder stile is reached on the right, where there is a signpost for Broadmeadows Youth Hostel. The track to the right descends in about 1.5km to the hostel, a simple rural YH, that lies a little above Yarrowfoot in the Yarrow Valley. In 2005 a windfarm had been proposed for the hills in this area. If given the go-ahead it will greatly disfigure this beautiful, tranquil landscape of rolling grassy Border hills.

If not overnighting at Broadmeadows, continue ahead along the SUW, now with a plantation on your left. Climb eastwards to the triangulation station (OS number plate S7570) on the summit of the **Three Brethren** (464m; 1522ft), a hill top named after the three enormous and expertly constructed stone cairns that crown the summit. A 360-degree panorama greets the eye on arriving at the cairns. Leave the Three Brethren on a good path that descends south-south-eastwards to the col between it and Peat Law (426m; 1397ft), where the path bends to the left to descend north-eastwards through the forest to reach the Tweed Valley at Yair.

The view to the north-east whilst on the descent towards Yair

On reaching a metalled lane at Yair turn right onto it, continuing the descent into the valley, to meet and follow the River Tweed. Turn left crossing the superb stone-arched bridge over the Tweed at Yair, after which turn right at **Fairnilee Farm**, at a signpost which indicates a public footpath to Galashiels. The track soon starts to ascend, first in trees and then crosses a metalled drive to continue the climb, now between fields. Pass the solitary building of Calfshaw, aiming for a prominent gap in the trees ahead on Hog Hill. Continue the ascent of the grassy hillside, following waymarker posts until you cross a stone stile in a dry stone wall (dyke) and begin the descent into Galashiels, the buildings of which are now clearly visible ahead. Eventually cross a stone stile to enter a wood. Descend on a good path through the trees to pass a wooden seat, from where there is a viewpoint through the trees to the three Eildon Hills above Melrose. Continue, reaching another stone stile at the end of the wood, and over this to descend a grassy field. Follow waymarker posts until you reach a tall stone wall by the edge of a wood.

The original line of the SUW has been 'realigned', from this point to the far side of Galashiels. The Way

152

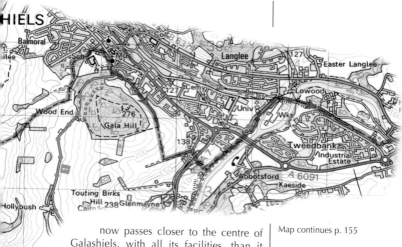

Map continues p. 155

now passes closer to the centre of Galashiels, with all its facilities, than it originally did. The route has to be followed quite carefully, as some of the waymarker posts on the author's visit had been vandalised or removed. The followed detailed notes should assist the walker.

Turn left over a stone stile (not the wooden one behind the wall) to walk along the edge of the wood, with a dry stone wall (dyke) on your right. Bear left in front of a gate (i.e. do **not** pass through the gate into the wood) to a kissing gate. Turn right through this gate with the wood now on your right. Turn left at a waymarker post by a large pine tree and soon right again at another marker post, down through the wood and follow the path as it bends to the left over a foot-bridge, after which bear right onto the main path. This leads to a road on the outskirts of **Galashiels** by the town swimming pool. Follow the signpost ahead for the town centre (reached in about 400m), but to continue on the SUW turn right to enter a town park adjacent to Galashiels Academy. In front of this school turn left and then right in front of the park toilets,

Equestrian statue outside the Town Hall, Galashiels

continuing ahead to pass to the right of Waverley old people's home, followed by the tall and elegant sandstone tower of St Paul's Church.

On reaching a T-junction turn left for 30m to a crossroads opposite Tea Street. Turn right here, uphill, as indicated by a SUW signpost. Turn left into Barr Road, rejoining the original route of the SUW, before its realignment through Galashiels. Where the metalled surface ends continue ahead on a path into the woods. The trail skirts the side of Gala Hill, with the buildings of suburban Galashiels down to the left in the Gala Water Valley. The path emerges from the wood at the corner of a field (benches) where there is both a wonderful view of the Eildon Hills and surrounding countryside, and a stone tablet with the inscription: 'Here Roger Quinn, author of *The Borderland,* gazed on Scotland's Eden from the spur of Gala Hill'. This poet, playwright and lover of the Border Hills was born on the 25th June 1850 and died in Dumfries on the 31st July 1925.

Descend the edge of a field southwards to a double gate and bench on the left, where you turn to head eastwards, still with a dry stone wall (dyke) on your left, to reach a road at Brunswickhill, on the edge of a housing estate. Bear left off the road onto a path that leads to a flight of wooden steps down to the A7. Cross this busy road with care to take the 'no through road' opposite. This leads down to the River Tweed. About 50m before this lane reaches the river, the official route takes a path down to the

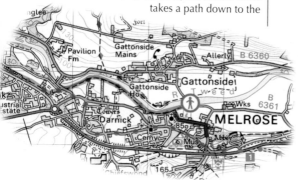

left to meet the river. If you would like a good riverside picnic spot with picnic tables then turn right, but for the SUW take the path opposite, down to the riverbank and turn left (north-east) alongside the river. The path eventually passes under the A6091 and then soon pulls away from the river, through woodland, to reach a road where you turn right across Gala Water Bridge and continue for about another 300m to turn right at a brightly coloured National Cycle network signpost.

The cycle route is along the course of an old disused railway line. Follow this until you reach a large knitwear factory (Barbour), where the Way bears slightly to the left to cross a main road at Lowood Nurseries (there is a bus stop for Melrose and Galashiels at this point). Now take a path that the SUW shares with the Borders Abbeys Way. It follows the River Tweed into **Melrose**. This attractive section of riverbank lined with many old and elegant deciduous trees is a popular walk with locals and families. Pass Melrose Bowling Club to arrive at a SUW Information Board at a weir on the river. The SUW continues to the Chain Bridge visible ahead, but for the facilities in the town and to visit **Melrose Abbey** (highly recommended) or to walk on the beautiful Eildon Hills, turn right at the Information Board, away from the river towards the town centre. The shortest walking route to reach the Abbey and Tourist Information Centre is to turn left at Melrose Rugby Football Club.

PLACES OF INTEREST

Drove Road

The route over Minch Moor to the Three Brethren uses an ancient drove road following the crest of a long line of hills stretching eastwards from Traquair. It has been used over the centuries by armies (Edward I brought his men over here in 1296), the monks of Kelso and of course drovers herding their charges to the English markets in the south.

Cheese Well

This is a small spring on Minch Moor, the source of the Plora Burn, which flows northwards. It gets its name from the tradition that in days gone by travellers would leave small pieces of cheese to placate the water spirits, who would then hopefully offer protection to the wayfarer.

Broadmeadows

Broadmeadows, opened in 1931, has the distinction of being the first-ever hostel in the Scottish Youth Hostels Association's network. After the opening ceremony a walk was made over Minch Moor and this was repeated on the hostel's 50-year anniversary in 1981. A kilometre away is Foulshiels, birthplace of the African explorer Mungo Park.

The Ridings

The Common Ridings or Ridings of the Marches are an annual custom in the Scottish Borders, as well as in parts of Dumfries & Galloway. Each town has its Ridings that take place every year in the springtime or summer. Neighbouring towns often have these events on different weekends in the season so as not to conflict and allow as many people as possible to enjoy the rides or to spectate. Often hundreds of horseriders take part with considerable pomp and pageantry riding the 'marches' or boundaries of the common land of the parishes or Burghs. The Ridings date from a time past when it was necessary to guard one's territory with care. Cairns were erected at several key boundary points, as at the Three Brethren.

The Three Brethren

This well-known summit of the Border Hills is crowned by three enormous cairns or 'stone men'. Three border fences come together here delineating the boundaries of the parishes of Philiphaugh, Selkirk and Yair that meet at this point, each parish laying claim to one of the Three Brethren cairns. It is one of the major focal points of the Selkirk Common Ridings in June.

The Yair Bridge over the River Tweed

The River Tweed

Perhaps Scotland's most famous Salmon river, the Tweed is encountered on the SUW on and off between Yair and Melrose. It is a Borders river, but its source lies in the Moffat Hills five miles north of the town, on the watershed to the north of the Devil's Beef Tub. The infant river at first travels northwards but it soon rapidly increases in width as it turns to head east, before finally draining into the North Sea at Berwick-on-Tweed in Northumberland. This very wide and gently flowing river is 156km (97 miles) long, and because of its diversity of habitat has been designated as an SSSI throughout its length.

Galashiels

One of the largest towns in the region Galashiels is known for its textile industry. There are tours of the Wool Centre where tartan is woven, but the main places of interest lie outside the town, notably at Abbotsford, Sir Walter Scott's house (see below). There is B&B accommodation in the town.

Melrose

Melrose is perhaps the most beautiful of the towns of the Scottish Borders and there is much to see and do here, easily filling a full day for any that wish for a day off from the Way. Apart from the famous Abbey ruins, the Eildon Hills, the graceful River Tweed and the nearby home of Sir Walter Scott, there are also two outstanding gardens to visit, Harmony Gardens and Priorwood Gardens, both National Trust for Scotland properties. Rugby fans will find interest in the Melrose Rugby Heritage Centre, as Melrose is the home of Rugby Sevens, the popular Borders game, founded in 1883. Finally, the Trimontium (Three Hills) exhibition a little way out of town gives insight into life here in Roman times at the site of a Roman signal station. A guided walk to Trimontium takes place once a week during the season.

The Chain Bridge over the River Tweed at Melrose, a suspension bridge for the use of pedestrians only, was opened on 26th October 1826. It was strengthened and reconstructed in 1991, having been repaired earlier in 1928. ▶

Melrose has a fine youth hostel and plenty of B&Bs, shops, cafes and restaurants.

A sign on the bridge states that: 'No more than 8 persons should be on the bridge at one time. Passengers are requested not to cross the bridge in a heavy gale'!

The Tourist Information Centre, Melrose

The Chain Bridge over the River Tweed, Melrose

Melrose Abbey

The Abbey was founded in 1136 by King David I and established by Cistercian monks from Rievaulx in Yorkshire. It was attacked, destroyed and rebuilt several times during its lifetime, the present ruins remaining after an attack in 1545. The ruins are thought by many to be the most picturesque and romantic of all the Borders Abbeys. The heart of Robert the Bruce is buried, so tradition holds, in the Abbey grounds.

Abbotsford

Situated halfway between Melrose and Galashiels, on the banks of the River Tweed, Abbotsford is a mecca for admirers of the 19th-century novelist Sir Walter Scott, who lived there for many years. The attractive property contains a large library and a collection of historic relics and weapons. The gardens are also very fine. The property is open daily from Easter to the end of October (admission charge). There is a tearoom on site.

Eildon Hills

The triplet of the Eildon Hills, a National Scenic Area above Melrose, form the most distinctive landmark in the Borders, and will be seen for several days from various high vantage points on the SUW. Although relatively low in stature and covering quite a small area, these volcanic plugs, because of their isolation from other hill ranges, form an easily recognisable skyline seen from afar. Said to be formed by an ancient wizard who split one hill into three, but in reality the Eildons are the result of complex volcanic activity. The famous viewpoint of the Eildons known as Scott's View lies a few miles to the east of Melrose on the B6356 above the River Tweed. This view was beloved of Sir Walter Scott and it is said that his favourite horse, that pulled his hearse on the way from Abbotsford to his burial site at Dryburgh Abbey, stopped at this point for Scott to say a last farewell to his beloved

The Eildon Hills rising steeply above the town of Melrose

hills of home. An afternoon exploring these grand little hills, which have fine viewpoints from every summit, would be time well spent. Two short and signposted Eildon Walks help visitors to make the most of their time on these hills. Eildon Mid Hill at 422m (1384ft) is the highest of the three hills, on either side of which lie Eildon North Hill (404m; 1325ft) and Eildon Wester (371m; 1217ft). The former is topped by an old Roman Signal Station and Hill Fort.

St Cuthbert's Way

This popular long-distance footpath links the Southern Upland Way at Melrose with Holy Island, Lindisfarne, on the north-east coast of England. Opened in 1996 St Cuthbert's Way makes an excellent alternative eastern termination to the SUW. It runs for 100km (62 miles) from Melrose (where St Cuthbert started his ministry in around AD650) to Lindisfarne on Holy Island where the saint, renowned for his healing powers, became Bishop. On the way the waymarked trail passes the Eildon Hills, Dryburgh Abbey, the River Tweed, the Roman road of Dere Street, the Cheviot Hills, the Northumberland Fell Sandstone Moors and the Lindisfarne National Nature Reserve. It passes through Kirk Yetholm, the northern terminus of the Pennine Way, and so forms a useful link between the SUW and the Pennine Way, two major National Trails. There is a guidebook to St Cuthbert's Way (see Appendix 2) and Harvey Maps have produced an excellent strip map of the trail. Up-to-date information is available from Melrose Tourist Information Centre (see Appendix 3).

Borders Abbeys Way

This 105km (65 mile) circular waymarked walking trail links the Borders Abbeys of Kelso, Jedburgh, Melrose and Dryburgh and includes the towns of Hawick and Selkirk. It meets the SUW at Melrose. After a delay of many years the trail is now complete. Free leaflets describing the route are available by sending a SAE to Melrose Tourist Information Centre (see Appendix 3).

STAGE 11

Melrose to Lauder

10.2 miles (16.4km)

	Distance (miles)		Distance (km)	
	Sectional	Cumulative	Sectional	Cumulative
Melrose	0	169.2	0	272.2
Gattonside	0.7	169.9	1.2	273.4
Easter Housebyres	1.6	171.5	2.5	275.9
Jeaniefield	4.0	175.5	6.4	282.3
Woodheads Hill (303m)	2.0	177.5	3.3	285.6
Lauder	1.9	179.4	3.0	288.6

Summary
A short stage only today, offering some time for a look around Melrose in the morning before setting out on the walk to Lauder. The Tweed is crossed at Melrose by a splendid old chain suspension footbridge before the town is left behind. This stage offers easy walking for the most part, along the line of a Roman road. It is pleasant, low level countryside, where many shades of green and brown are on display in the patchwork of fields that spread before the eye on either side of the trail.

Route
To start the day's walk return to the SUW Information Board on the bank of the River Tweed in **Melrose**, a short distance upstream from Melrose Chain Bridge. Continue along the riverbank to cross this quite spectacular footbridge, so leaving the Borders Abbeys Way at this point. Now follow the northern (Gattonside) bank of the River Tweed westwards. The path eventually climbs to leave the riverbank and reach a road where the route continues ahead. After about 250m turn right off this road onto a grassy track, so beginning the climb over the hills to Lauder.

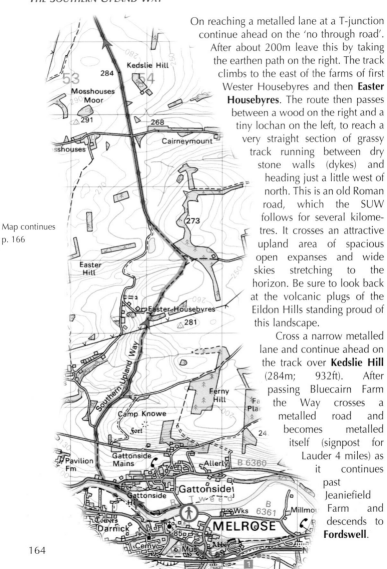

On reaching a metalled lane at a T-junction continue ahead on the 'no through road'. After about 200m leave this by taking the earthen path on the right. The track climbs to the east of the farms of first Wester Housebyres and then **Easter Housebyres**. The route then passes between a wood on the right and a tiny lochan on the left, to reach a very straight section of grassy track running between dry stone walls (dykes) and heading just a little west of north. This is an old Roman road, which the SUW follows for several kilometres. It crosses an attractive upland area of spacious open expanses and wide skies stretching to the horizon. Be sure to look back at the volcanic plugs of the Eildon Hills standing proud of this landscape.

Cross a narrow metalled lane and continue ahead on the track over **Kedslie Hill** (284m; 932ft). After passing Bluecairn Farm the Way crosses a metalled road and becomes metalled itself (signpost for Lauder 4 miles) as it continues past Jeaniefield Farm and descends to **Fordswell**.

Map continues p. 166

164

Here the SUW leaves the narrow metalled lane by taking a track on the left around a small wood. It continues north-north-west dead straight, soon passing under high tension electricity cables held on huge pylons, before climbing to the summit of **Woodheads Hill** (303m; 994ft). Here the Way crosses a road. Right leads to Lauder by this road, but the SUW continues ahead, with wall and wood on your right. The trail begins to drop towards Lauder, which lies in the deeply cut valley ahead, but before it does so it crosses a ladder stile and climbs to the right to reach, rather surprisingly, the 13th tee of a golf course!

The SUW passes this churchyard on its approach to Lauder High Street

The path follows the boundary fence of Lauder Golf Course, with Lauder Water down below left and Lauder itself soon coming into view. You will reach a wooden

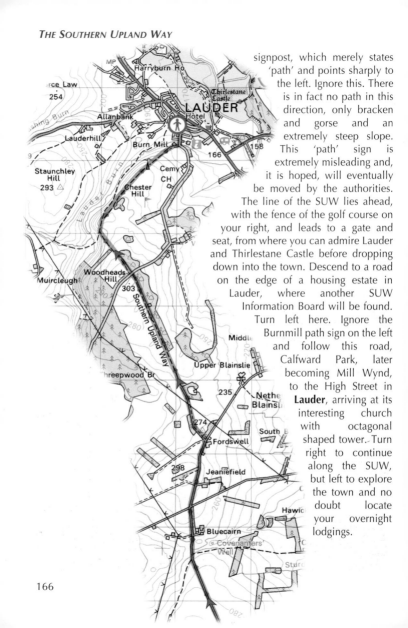

signpost, which merely states 'path' and points sharply to the left. Ignore this. There is in fact no path in this direction, only bracken and gorse and an extremely steep slope. This 'path' sign is extremely misleading and, it is hoped, will eventually be moved by the authorities. The line of the SUW lies ahead, with the fence of the golf course on your right, and leads to a gate and seat, from where you can admire Lauder and Thirlestane Castle before dropping down into the town. Descend to a road on the edge of a housing estate in Lauder, where another SUW Information Board will be found. Turn left here. Ignore the Burnmill path sign on the left and follow this road, Calfward Park, later becoming Mill Wynd, to the High Street in **Lauder**, arriving at its interesting church with octagonal shaped tower. Turn right to continue along the SUW, but left to explore the town and no doubt locate your overnight lodgings.

PLACES OF INTEREST

Gattonside
On the north side of the Tweed this developed area was once orchards for the monks of the abbey at Melrose.

Roman Road
The section from Gattonside to Lauder uses for the most part the line of a Roman road that went northwards towards Lauderdale from their signal station at Trimontium. It offers some fast and generally easy walking.

The Black Bull, High Street Lauder

Lauder

The Royal and Ancient Burgh of Lauder is the principal town of Lauderdale, the valley of Leader Water, the present A68 which runs through the town being the oldest established route between the Scottish capital and England. Its origins are probably Roman but it was first recorded (as 'Lawedir') in the 12th century when it is believed to have been given its Royal Burgh status, one of the first in Scotland. Lauder has the dubious distinction of having had the first of the Covenanter martyrs, the minister of the Kirk, who was executed for his beliefs in Edinburgh in 1661. The main street is wide, forming a market place dominated by the old Town Hall with clocktower. The few narrow back lanes and neat atmosphere make Lauder a charming small town. ◀ There is hotel and B&B accommodation for the visitor, and several cafes, pubs, restaurants and shops in the town. The Black Bull on the High Street can be particularly recommended for its fine food. For Thirlestane House and Gardens see under 'Places of Interest' for Stage 12.

Visitors can become better acquainted with the town by walking the 2km long 'town trail': information plaques are located at numbered sites of interest along the route.

Lauder Common Riding was one of the original Ridings of the Marches and takes place on the first Saturday every August after a week of festivities. The elected town's 'Cornet' carries the Burgh Standard, followed by many other horsemen and women, around the boundaries of the Burgh.

Sir Walter Scott Way

Leaflets and other publicity may be seen describing a 92 mile (148km) long-distance walk from Moffat to Cockburnspath, entitled the Sir Walter Scott Way. Do not be fooled into believing that this is a new or a different path. Although no mention of the fact is usually made in the literature, this walk for the most part uses the SUW, except for an optional alternative section from the Three Brethren to Selkirk and on to Melrose via Abbotsford.

STAGE 12

Lauder across the Lammermuir Hills to Longformacus

15.4 miles (24.8km)

| | Distance (miles) | | Distance (km) | |
	Sectional	Cumulative	Sectional	Cumulative
Lauder	0	179.4	0	288.6
A697 (Wanton Walls)	1.3	180.7	2.1	290.7
Braidshawrig	4.5	185.2	7.3	298.0
Twin Law (447m)	4.0	189.2	6.5	304.5
Watch Water Reservoir (Dam)	2.9	192.1	4.6	309.1
Rawburn	1.1	193.2	1.8	310.9
Longformacus	1.6	194.8	2.5	313.4

Summary
Today's stage is essentially a long crossing of the Lammermuir Hills, but it begins with a gentle walk through the parkland of Thirlestane Estate, with the opportunity to visit its castle and gardens. After crossing the A697 the SUW commences a 20km (12.4 mile) traverse of the lonely, heathery upland moorland of the Lammermuirs. As these moors are so featureless and windswept, this section demands respect, particularly in poor weather conditions. The highlight of this long traverse is the highest point on the crossing, the conspicuous two large cairns that adorn the summit of Twin Law (447m; 1466ft). This grand viewpoint is a good spot for lunch or for an afternoon snack stop during fine, warm and clear weather conditions, before descending to Watch Water Reservoir, a favourite haunt of anglers. The crossing of the Lammermuirs is completed with a descent into the tranquil village of Longformacus, where there are two or three B&B establishments offering overnight accommodation.

Route

Walk south-eastwards out of town along **Lauder** High Street, the A68. On the outskirts of the town turn left off this main road at a SUW and 'Herring Road to Dunbar' signpost, passing between two large red gateposts and descending into Thirlestane Park. Descend to a finger-post. Right is to Thirlestane Campsite, left is to the entrance of **Thirlestane Castle and Gardens**, a visit to which can be recommended. But the SUW takes the track ahead to cross the river (Leader Water) by means of a footbridge. Follow the thistle waymarks carefully across this parkland to a gate and stile. The path soon climbs up to a kissing gate, with Drummond's Hall, private, to the left. Turn right here on a grassy track that leads to the A697 road at **Wanton Walls**.

Cross this main road with care to follow the surfaced drive ahead. Turn left immediately after a large barn to pass the

Map continues p. 172

farmhouse and take the track that leads from it up towards the woods. Pass a water filter station and later water storage tanks, before entering woodland. ▶ Turn right at a track T-junction to exit the trees, where you take a left fork to begin a long traverse of the Lammermuir Hills.

The route heads north-north-east passing close to point 336, marked on the OS Landranger map, east of **Edgarhope Wood**, before descending to cross Snawdon Burn. Take time to follow the SUW marker posts carefully in this area. Diligence is required to stay on the correct line of the route. Do not cross a cattle grid into an arable field,

Be sure to look back before entering the trees to enjoy the view down to Lauder in the valley below and of the Eildon Hills in the distance to the south.

Braidshawrig Farm

but climb over the stile by a fieldgate to its left. Follow a wall on the right, noting the stone seat built into the wall after a few metres, to another stile. Cross this to turn right, now with another wall on your right. Go over another stile next to a fieldgate and ahead north-eastwards over the shoulder of **Heugh Hill** to descend towards Blythe Water. On clear days the footbridge over the river, which was constructed by Queen's University OTC in 1993, is seen from some distance; cross a stile in a fence to drop down to cross the bridge, taking the track that scars the hillside opposite.

Climb a stile in a dry stone wall (dyke), heading north-east for the right-hand edge of the small conifer plantation seen ahead. The lowland fields have now given way to vast acres of heather- and bracken-covered moorland and upland pasture for sheep and cattle. Follow the edge of the plantation until you reach a track at a cattle grid where there is a wide gap in the trees. Turn left to follow the track through this gap and continue north along the track to **Braidshawrig**. Bear left in front of this lonely farmhouse to climb eastwards away from Easter Burn. Remain on this track for a further 4.5km. The twin cairns on the summit of

Twin Law (447m; 1466ft) will be seen ahead to the right for a long time before they are eventually reached, assuming hill fog is not blanketing these moors. The track comes to an abrupt end on a shallow ridge, a little over 1.5km north-west of Twin Law. Turn right onto a good path. The reservoir of Watch Water will now be visible down to the left. The path leads all the way to the two huge cairns and trig station (number plate S7524) on the summit.

Watch Water Reservoir is clearly seen, conditions permitting, below to the east, and this is our next destination. Leave the summit on the clear path that heads eastwards from the East Cairn. The path descends a broad ridge towards the reservoir to reach a crossing track in a wide hollow. Turn left on this grassy track to descend and cross

Watch Water (footbridge to left of the track). About 200m after the stream turn right at a SUW fingerpost indicating the way to Longformacus. Pass the farm of **Scarlaw**, after which the track becomes surfaced as it traverses above the north shore of the reservoir to reach its dam. The public road starts at the far end of the dam. Follow it over the hill to **Rawburn Farm** and then on down to **Longformacus**. In the latter stages of this walk the road follows Dye Water which leads into the village. The SUW arrives in the village opposite Longformacus

Watch Water Reservoir seen from Scarlow

Church and alongside the stone arched bridge over Dye Water. Turn left to visit the village, but right to continue along the SUW.

PLACES OF INTEREST

Thirlestane Castle and Gardens

Thirlestane Castle is of the finest stately homes in Scotland. Its origins lie in the 13th century, but it was re-built for the Maitland family in the 16th century and this family is still in residency today, although the castle has been extended and improved since that time. It is the seat of the Earls and Duke of Lauderdale, and several of its 98 rooms as well as the gardens and grounds are open to the public. The many towers and turrets of the building give a fairytale appearance to the castle. Note that the last admission is at 2.30pm, which is not convenient for SUW walkers who might otherwise visit it in the afternoon, after a morning's walk from Melrose. Thirlestane Castle is open from 1st May to the middle of September for 4 days a week, but every day except Saturday in July and August (admission charge).

The Lammermuirs

The Lammermuir Hills ('Lamb's Moor') are the most north-easterly tops of the Southern Uplands of Scotland, an upland barrier between Lothian and the coast in the north and the Borders to the south. An extensive rather featureless area of high moorland, with relatively few distinctive summits, it warrants particular care in navigation, even on the SUW, especially over the first section before the track leading to Braidshawrig is reached. In conditions of dense hill fog, high winds and/or continuous heavy rain with low visibility, only the experienced, navigationally competent and well equipped should set out across these moors. Winter blizzards can be abominable.

East Cairn, Twin Law, Lammermuir Hills

The SUW includes just one of the Lammermuir hills, Twin Law (447m; 1466ft), but it is the range's most distinctive, an extensive summit viewpoint that is topped by two enormous cairns that stand about 50m apart and are visible for miles around. The western cairn is the broader of the two. Both have been expertly constructed from carefully selected stones and both have a small alcove and stone seat on their southern flanks. There may be a logbook here to enter your visit. Judging by the entries in these books the cairns have been used as 'howffs' (primitive shelters in the hills) by some hardy SUW walkers. Legend has it that the cairns represent two brothers who lost contact with each other in childhood, joined opposing armies and mortally wounded each other in the mythical Battle of Twinlaw. A poem in local dialect, inscribed on a plaque on the triangulation pillar on the summit, confirms this story. ◄

This trig pillar is maintained in pristine condition by the Gullane Walking Club who adopted it in 1994, when the Ordnance Survey no longer required its use.

Other hills in the range include Dirrington Great Law (398m; 1305ft) and Dirrington Little Law (363m; 1191ft) both seen to good effect from the Way, and Lammer Law (527m; 1729ft) and Meikle Says Law (535m; 1755ft), the latter being the highest point on the Lammermuirs. For more walks in the Lammermuirs see the excellent leaflet entitled 'Walking in the Lammermuir Hills' produced by the Scottish Rights of Way and Access Society (see Appendix 3) and their Scottish Hill Tracks publication (see Appendix 2).

The Lammermuir Hills have a peculiar distinction in that they are the only range of hills in Britain to form the background to a romantic Italian opera, Lucia di Lammermoor (Lucy of Lammermuir) by Donizetti!

The Herring Road

This is an ancient route across the Lammermuir Hills from the herring fisheries on the Lothian coast at Dunbar to Lauder and beyond. Salted herring was carried on this trail and 17th-century reports indicate that the industry was very considerable indeed. Deep grooves in the paths can be seen in places made by the vast numbers of heavily laden pack animals that once trod these trade routes. The SUW makes use of the Herring Way between Lauder and Watch Water Reservoir, from where the Herring Road takes its leave to head northwards to Dye Cottage, Whiteadder Reservoir and the Lothian coast.

Longformacus

An attractive village with a high stone bridge over the river, the Dye Water, that rises in the Lammermuir Hills to the west. The church dates from 1234. The B&B establishments are an essential service for SUW walkers before setting out on the last stage of their journey to the east coast. Properties in the village are much sought after by people retiring from the south and by commuters to the offices of Edinburgh, which is surprisingly close, although it is a still a world away to the SUW walker.

Longformacus

STAGE 13

Longformacus to Cockburnspath

17.2 miles (27.7km)

	Distance (miles)		Distance (km)	
	Sectional	Cumulative	Sectional	Cumulative
Longformacus	0	194.8	0	313.4
B 6355 (Lodge Wood)	3.6	198.4	5.9	319.3
Abbey St Bathans	3.2	201.6	5.1	324.4
A1	5.6	207.2	9.0	333.4
Pease Dean Wildlife Reserve	2.6	209.8	4.2	337.6
Cove Village	1.5	211.3	2.4	340.0
Cockburnspath	0.7	212.0	1.1	341.1

Summary
The Last Stage
The high hills and moorland of the Southern Uplands are now all behind and to the west of the SUW walker, and this final section offers mainly easy walking through some of the rich arable farming country that lies to the south of Edinburgh. There are one or two hills still to climb, but none of these offer major obstacles to progress towards the east coast. From Longformacus the route crosses over some low hills before following a pleasant woodland track high above the Whiteadder valley to reach the little hamlet of Abbey St Bathans, with its historic and picturesque church. A succession of rich arable fields come after Abbey St Bathans until the A1 'Great North Road' is reached. More woodland walking follows, but with the first good close-up view of the east coast excitement may grow as Pease Bay is approached by a walk through Pease Dean Wildlife Reserve.

The SUW finishes with a little over a kilometre of first-rate coastal walking, along the tops of the high cliffs between Pease Bay and the tiny village of Cove. A detour

Abbey Church at Abbey St Bathans

down to the little gem of Cove Harbour is strongly recommended, as this is the spiritual end of the SUW, a small picturesque harbour, perhaps a minuscule version of Portpatrick on the west coast, where this adventure all started a couple of weeks ago. Although to the tired but exultant SUW 'completer' it will doubtless feel that this venture began many lifetimes ago! But the actual end of the SUW is still nearly a kilometre inland, at the rather uninspiring village of Cockburnspath, where there is an ancient market cross and the last SUW Information Board, which proclaims this point to be the end of the Southern Upland Way. Alas Cockburnspath is no Portpatrick, but Cove Harbour is much more comparable. Like Portpatrick pretty Cove Harbour has been used for cinema and TV films. Some scenes from the Judi Dench and Billy Connolly film of 'Mrs Brown', depicting a part of the life of Queen Victoria, were shot here.

A bus from Cockburnspath will take you north to Dunbar and Edinburgh, or south to Berwick-on-Tweed and Newcastle. You will thus be quickly returned to 'normal life'.

Route

Head south-east on the road out of **Longformacus.** After about 200m of uphill walking, just after a SUW Information Board, turn left on a lane signposted to Whitchester. After about 1.3km there is a small alteration from the original line of the SUW, which took a route to the right a few metres after the bridge over the Blacksmill Burn. Continue on the lane for a further 200m or so to a small kink in the road, where a new SUW fingerpost will be found. Turn right over the stile here to climb up the field with a fence on your left. The well-defined route heads eastwards; note the cone of Dirrington Great Law dominating the landscape to the south-west. Continue uphill on the south-east side of Owl Hill (missing out Commonside, which was included in the old route), and then follow the left side of a narrow stretch of woodland. After about 300m cut through this thin strip of woodland, so rejoining the original route at a SUW fingerpost.

Right for 50m here leads to a viewpoint, but the SUW turns left, north. The views out to sea on the north-east coast of southern Scotland, first glimpsed from Twin Law, are now

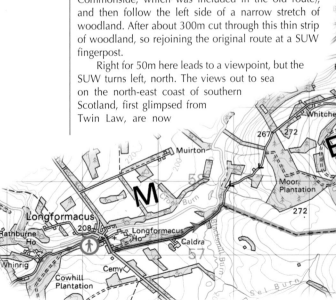

extensive. A track descends through grassland and then through **Lodge Wood** to meet the B6355 road. Turn left on this road for about 150m to take a track that

Map continues p. 183

climbs steeply on the right, soon hair-pinning to the left to climb beside a thin strip of conifers. After the track levels leave it on a narrow path on the right, at a SUW waymarker post. The trail crosses the head of a deep cleft above **Ellemford Bridge**, before eventually descending very steeply, by a flight of grass-covered steps, to meet a track at the edge of woodland. Turn right onto this track, which skirts around Abbey Hill, high above Whiteadder Water valley below. This most pleasant of woodland tracks eventually descends to the level of the river, follows it for a while, and ascends a little before finally descending to reach the road at **Abbey St Bathans.**

Cross the road at a phone box to pass the church and cross the long footbridge over Whiteadder Water. On the far side of the river there is

SUW Information Board at Cockburnspath, the End of the SUW

another short route change from the original line of the SUW. The official Way now turns right alongside the river. After about 350m, cross a wooden footbridge over a tributary, but at a second bridge, this one of metal, at a cross-tracks, turn left signposted for Cockburnspath, and do not cross the metal bridge. This lane soon become a track which follows the course of the stream, first to the north-north-east and then to the north-west to climb a bank to a stile and fieldgate, where you turn right uphill on a footpath, heading for a pylon. Bear left at the top to follow a dry stone wall (dyke) on your right to reach a SUW fingerpost, where the original route is rejoined.

Follow the grassy path beneath the high-tension power lines, heading north to pass a large cairn topped by a red cock weathervane. The cairn and weathervane were constructed to celebrate a hundred years of occupation of **Whiteburn Farm** by the Cockburn family, from 1848 to 1948. But these days Whiteburn Farm is a 4x4 off-road training centre, which also offers quad bike trekking. The route of the SUW has been realigned here to avoid this property. So bear left at the 'SUW No access

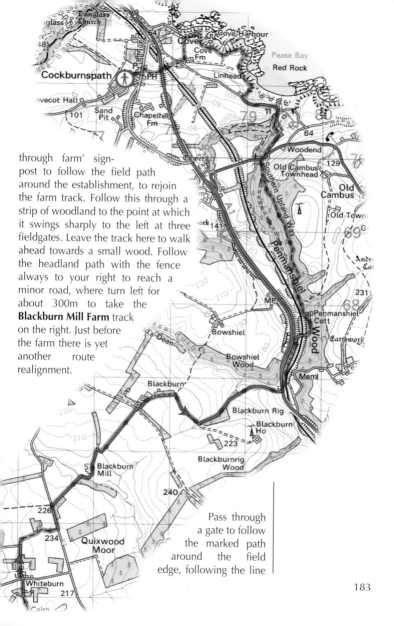

through farm' signpost to follow the field path around the establishment, to rejoin the farm track. Follow this through a strip of woodland to the point at which it swings sharply to the left at three fieldgates. Leave the track here to walk ahead towards a small wood. Follow the headland path with the fence always to your right to reach a minor road, where turn left for about 300m to take the **Blackburn Mill Farm** track on the right. Just before the farm there is yet another route realignment.

Pass through a gate to follow the marked path around the field edge, following the line of the track past the farm, but on the other side of a hedge. The field path re-emerges on the track, which is now followed ahead to Blackburn Farm.

The SUW joins a public road at a row of terraced houses. Follow this road for just over 1.5km, descending to the A1. Cross this major trunk road where indicated with great care, and then follow the grassy path between the A1 on your left and the railway line (main line to Edinburgh) on your right. This soon leads to a section of the old A1 road which is followed ahead until you turn right over Bridge No. 117 over the railway line. Turn left to follow a grassy path through woodland to the right of a small stream. After a few hundred metres, soon after a short rise, be sure to turn very sharply to the right, at an angle of almost 180 degrees, to begin an ascent. This junction is easily missed. If you do miss it then the path you are already on also leads to the A1107, but without the sea views (and without the ascent!).

Looking down to Cove Harbour from the coastal path

The official SUW route first climbs to the south-south-east before hair-pinning left to continue the ascent to the north-north-west. A level stretch follows, and then, just before the steep descent commences, extensive views open out of the coastline to the north; particularly evident is Torness Power Station, Barns Ness lighthouse, the Bass Rock in the Firth of Forth, and the Fife peninsula north of Edinburgh. ▶ About 150m later be sure not to miss a thin path descending by wooden railings on the left to a splendid arched railway bridge at the A1107.

The path descends to join up with the non-official low level route that comes in from the left, where you will emerge if you miss the turn-off detailed above.

Turn right along this road for 20m to take a grassy path on the left, to enter Pease Dean Wildlife Reserve. Long flights of wooden steps lead down to a SUW Information Board near the coast at **Pease Bay**. Cross the river by a footbridge and turn right to ascend a flight of wooden steps to a road at Pease Bay Holiday Home Park. Turn left uphill on this road for about 500m to a point above the west end of Pease Bay. Turn right at the SUW fingerpost to begin a splendid walk along these coastal cliffs.

The route passes through a kissing gate on the right (easily missed), crosses a stream and climbs a flight of wooden steps to attain the coastal path. Follow the path above the cliffs for a little over a kilometre. Do take care on these cliff tops. This beautiful stretch of coast is marred only by the serried ranks of caravans in Pease Bay. The coastal path passes above Cove Harbour and eventually comes to a kissing gate where there is a signpost indicating the SUW to the left and **Cove Harbour** to the right. ▶ An interesting tunnel leads to the landward side of the harbour and in Cove village there is an interpretative board explaining the history of Cove and its harbour.

The latter is a very worthwhile short detour.

After you have enjoyed a visit to Cove Harbour return to the SUW signpost, pass through the kissing gate and follow the grassy path south away from the coast. Cross a track to reach and cross a minor road. The trail passes first under the railway line and then the A1 and continues to the old A1 on the outskirts of **Cockburnspath**. Turn left for about 80m and then right at a SUW seat and Information Board that announces the fact that this is Cockburnspath, the End of the Southern

185

Upland Way. This is the place to take your celebratory photographs. Well done.

PLACES OF INTEREST

Abbey St Bathans

A rural idyll, a charming little village well away from any main roads, beside the babbling Whiteadder Water. There was once a Cistercian priory here. The church is worth a short visit before crossing the elegant suspension footbridge over the River.

Pease Dean Wildlife Reserve

Maintained by the Scottish Wildlife Trust whose aim it is to replace all conifers and non-native sycamore in the reserve with native oak and ash, to improve the area as a haven for wildlife. The deep gully of Pease Dean is crossed by a bridge 36m above the river, built in 1783. The beauty of the area is diminished by Pease Bay Holiday Home Park, a dreadful blot on this coastal landscape.

Cove Harbour

The two main rocks in Cove Harbour are called Red or Hollow Rock and Long Rock. The 60-metre long access tunnel to the bay was cut through the rock in the 18th century.

Cockburnspath

In order not to make a social blunder here it is important to learn that the name of the village is pronounced in the same way as a well-known brand of port i.e. as 'coe-burnspath', the 'coe' as in Glencoe – the 'ck' is most definitely not pronounced! There is one grocery shop in the village, open every day. This shop is in the village square, opposite the Cockburnspath Mercat Cross, which was erected in 1503 by James IV of Scotland in celebration of his marriage to Princess Margaret Tudor, a sister of Henry VIII. There is a bus stop in Cockburnspath and some B&B establishments.

The footbridge over White Adder
Water, Abbey St Bathans

APPENDIX 1

BOTHIES ALONG THE SUW

Six open and unmanned bothies are situated along the SUW. These buildings, which are permanently unlocked, provide basic shelter for all, whether SUW walkers or other countryside users. You may use them for overnight stops, or to shelter from inclement weather during the daytime. There are wooden sleeping areas, but no beds, bunks or mattresses. A table and some chairs are often provided, but there are few other facilities.

No toilets are provided, but there is normally a spade in the bothy: use this! Never defecate in the vicinity of the bothy; it is recommended that a hole of about 15cm is dug at least 200m from the bothy, and at least 60m from running water. After defecating back-fill the hole with soil. Burn (only in the bothy fire) or carry out used toilet paper.

It is most important to leave the bothy clean and tidy after your stay. Vandalism is a problem in some bothies from time to time, and on occasion a thoughtless bothy user leaves a door open so that the building is despoiled by animals. If you find a bothy in a vandalised or in an otherwise uninhabitable state, please report the fact to a SUW Ranger or to the Mountain Bothies Association (a contact telephone number will usually be found in the bothy). Similarly, if you discover any structural or other problems (leaky roof, damaged floorboards, stonework, missing roof tiles, broken windowpanes, etc) then please also report the fact.

The Beehive, Polskeoch and Minch Moor bothies have no fireplace. A fire may be lit in the other bothies if fuel is available, but do not cut down live tree branches to burn on the fire.

For an overnight stop in a bothy all equipment will be required that is normally used for camping, except that a tent, of course, will not be needed. So be sure to have sleeping bag, a 'Thermorest' or insulating mat, and stove with pans, utensils and fuel. A candle or torch is useful. Mice often tend to be frequent residents or visitors of bothies, so it is essential to protect food supplies from contamination (food is best hung if possible in a bag from a rafter).

Four of the bothies on the SUW are maintained by the Mountain Bothies Association (MBA), founded in 1965 'to maintain simple shelters in remote country for the benefit of all who love wild and lonely places'. Most of the maintenance work on MBA bothies is undertaken by members on a voluntary basis, in the form of 'work parties'. Membership is open to all (Appendix 3) but it is not

Polskeoch Bothy (Stage 5)

necessary to be an MBA member to use the bothies. In all the MBA maintains over a hundred bothies situated in the Highlands, Islands and Southern Uplands of Scotland, as well as several in Northern England and Wales.

'Bothying' along the SUW provides an enjoyable, albeit primitive, experience that will probably provide happy memories for many years to come. For some it may be but the start of a lifetime of exploring the wild and remote parts of this country and beyond, by making use of other similar primitive accommodation.

The Bothy Code
- Respect other users.
- Respect the bothy.
- Respect the surroundings.
- Conserve fuel. Never cut live wood.
- Leave no litter: carry out all rubbish that cannot be burnt in the bothy fire.
- Ensure the fire is out and the door properly closed when you leave.

Bothies are used entirely at your own risk.

Bothies serving the Southern Upland Way are listed here in order from west to east along the Way. The bothies maintained by the MBA are distinguished by (MBA) at the end of the bothy name. Note that there are no bothies situated at the eastern end of the SUW, for the last 60 miles of the Way. This is because there are more opportunities for finding accommodation at regular intervals from Traquair eastwards, as the SUW passes through or close to a number of towns and villages offering facilities that are less frequently encountered further west.

The Beehive
Grid Reference: NX 221715 (OS Landranger 76).
Near Laggangarn (Dumfries & Galloway – Stage 3).
On the route of the SUW.
27.6 miles (44.4km) from Portpatrick by the SUW.
A unique wooden construction in the shape of a 'beehive', built by the
    architect Charles Gulland as one of his 'all round buildings' in 1993/94.
No fireplace.
Opened in 1994.

White Laggan (MBA)
Grid Reference: NX 466775 (OS Landranger 77).
South of Loch Dee (Dumfries & Galloway – Stage 4).
0.3 mile (0.5km) off-route of the SUW.
The turn-off for the bothy from the SUW is 51.1 miles (82.2km) from
    Portpatrick by the SUW.
Opened in 1971.
Local contact: Sandy White, Forest Ranger, ☎ 01671 402420.

Polskeoch Bothy (Chalk Memorial Bothy)
Grid Reference: NS 686019 (OS Landranger 77).
Near Polskeoch, north-eastern end of the Water of Ken (Dumfries & Galloway –
    Stage 5).
On the route of the SUW.
81.4 miles (131.1km) from Portpatrick by the SUW.
This is a very comfortable bothy, with a table, armchairs and sleeping platform,
    but also there are pictures on the wall, and a bookshelf well supplied with
    books and other reading material.
No fireplace.
Opened in 1986.
Note that Manquhill Bothy at grid reference NX 671945, east of Manquhill Hill,
    is closed and no longer managed by the MBA.

Brattleburn (MBA)

Grid Reference: NT 016069 (OS Landranger 78).

East of Daer Reservoir (Dumfries & Galloway – Stage 7).

0.2 miles (0.35km) off-route of the SUW.

The turn-off for the bothy from the SUW is 112.7 miles (181.4km) from
   Portpatrick by the SUW.

Wood burning stove, chairs, a table and a sleeping area.

Opened in 1984.

Over Phawhope (MBA)

Grid Reference: NT 182082 (OS Landranger 79).

North-east of Ettrick Head (Scottish Borders – Stage 8).

On the route of the SUW.

128.6 miles (207km) from Portpatrick by the SUW.

Opened in 1982.

Local contact: Ronald Lamb, Fountain Forestry, ☎ 01848 331218.

Inside Over Phawhope Bothy (Stage 8)

Minch Moor (MBA)
Grid Reference: NT 342337 (OS Landranger 73).
South-east of Traquair (Scottish Borders – Stage 10).
On the route of the SUW.
153 miles (246.3km) from Portpatrick by the SUW.
A small wooden cabin built by the Scottish Border Rangers. Four Bunks only.
No fireplace.
Local contact: Mike Baker, Ranger, ☎ 01578 730239.

Distances between the Bothies
The following information will be particularly useful to those people wishing to make full use of the bothies available along the SUW:

Portpatrick > 27.6 miles (44.4km) > Beehive > 23.5 miles (37.8km) > White Laggan* > 30.4 miles (48.9km) > Polskeoch > 31.2 miles (50.3km) > Brattleburn* > 15.9 miles (25.6km) > Over Phawhope > 24.4 miles (39.3km) > Minch Moor > 59.0 miles (95.1km) > Cockburnspath.

* White Laggan and Brattleburn bothies are both slightly off-route of the SUW, so a short additional distance has to be walked to reach the bothy, and again to resume the route after the bothy visit. The distances given here are to the turn-off points from the SUW to these bothies. The other four bothies lie on the route of the SUW itself.

For those walkers wanting to spend as many nights as possible in bothies along the SUW, the only two bothies a moderately comfortable distance apart are Brattleburn and Over Phawhope bothies. Beehive Bothy to White Laggan Bothy and Over Phawhope to Minch Moor Bothy would be possible by very strong walkers, but White Laggan to Polskeoch and Polskeoch to Brattleburn are out of the question in one day for all but ultra-fit fellrunners.

APPENDIX 2

BIBLIOGRAPHY

The Southern Uplands by K. M. Andrew. Scottish Mountaineering Club District Guide. Second Edition 1992. The authoritative SMC guide to hillwalking in southern Scotland.

Scottish Hill Tracks. Scottish Rights of Way and Access Society. Fourth Edition (revised) 2004. The definitive guide to over three hundred hill tracks, old roads and rights of way throughout Scotland.

Walking the Galloway Hills by Paddy Dillon. Cicerone Press, 1995.

Walking in the Lowther Hills by Ronald Turnbull. Cicerone Press, 1999.

The Border Country, A Walker's Guide by Alan Hall. Cicerone Press, 1993.

Border Pubs and Inns, A Walker's Guide by Alan Hall. Cicerone Press, 2004.

Walks in the Lammermuirs by Alan Hall. Cicerone Press, 1996.

Southern Upland Way, Western Section – Short Walks. Dumfries & Galloway Ranger Service. Free. Thirty walks are described ranging from 1.5 to 20 miles in length.

Short Walks Guide to the Eastern Section of the Southern Upland Way. VisitScotland Borders. Free.

Along the Southern Upland Way by Jimmie Macgregor. BBC Books, 1990. Now out of print this little book written by one of Scotland's most popular celebrities is still to be found in many local libraries. Not a guide to the Way but a travelogue of the places visited and people encountered by Jimmie on the route.

The Southern Uplands. South of Scotland – Coast to Coast. Southern Uplands Partnership, 2005. A small nicely illustrated hardback book detailing the geology and geography of the hill country of southern Scotland and the human activities of those who live, work and visit there.

Highways & Byways in Galloway & Carrick by C. H. Dick. Originally published in 1916. C. H. Dick Memorial edition 2001 (G. C. Book Publishers, Wigtown). If you only wish to own one book on the south-west of Scotland then this is the one to choose, even though it was researched by means of bicycle and written at the time of the First World War by a clergyman. The style and scholarship is of a bygone age and a joy to read, but much of the information on the history and archaeology and topography of the area is still as it was nearly a century ago. The work has been brought to a modern audience by a facsimile re-publication at the beginning of the 21st century, where the original atmospheric line drawings of Hugh Thomson have been faithfully reproduced.

Writing the Way. A collection of articles to celebrate the 21st Anniversary of the SUW, by people who have walked the Way since it was opened in 1984. Available from The Southern Uplands Way Partnership, GCAT, High Street, New Galloway DG7 3RN or online at **www.southernuplandway.com**

From the Pennines to the Highlands, A walking route through the Scottish Borders by Hamish Brown, Lochar Publishing, 1992. Written by one of Scotland's most well-known hillwalkers this book, now sadly out of print, is a delight. Hamish has chosen an excellent route for this jaunt linking Byrness on the Pennine Way to Milngavie at the start of the West Highland Way. The book is packed with interesting snippets of information, told with an infectious enthusiasm by a man whose deep love for his country is plainly evident.

A Way to Whithorn by Andrew Patterson. Saint Andrew Press (1991). Out of print.

St Cuthbert's Way – the Official Guide by Roger Smith and Ron Shaw (Mercat Press, 1997).

Borders Abbeys Way. A series of five leaflets describe the route. Scottish Borders Council. Available from local Tourist Information Centres (see Appendix 3)

APPENDIX 3

USEFUL ADDRESSES, TELEPHONE NUMBERS AND WEBSITES

---

1. Tourist Offices in Dumfries & Galloway and in the Borders of most use to Southern Upland Way Walkers:

Stranraer Tourist Information Centre (open all year)
28 Harbour Street
☎ 01776 702595

Newton Stewart Tourist Information Centre (open Easter to October only)
Dashwood Square
☎ 01671 402431

Castle Douglas Tourist Information Centre (open Easter to October only)
Market Hill, King Street
☎ 01556 502611

Dumfries Tourist Information Centre (open all year: the main Tourist Office for the whole Dumfries & Galloway Region)
64, Whitesands, Dumfries DG1 2RS
☎ 01387 253862

Moffat Tourist Information Centre (open Easter to October only)
Churchgate, Moffat
☎ 01683 220620

VisitScotland Borders (open all year)
The main Tourist Information Centre in the Borders for telephone and postal enquiries.
Shepherd's Mill, Whinfield Road, Selkirk TD7 5DT
☎ 0870 608 0404

Peebles Tourist Information Centre (open all year)
High Street, Peebles EH45 8AG

Selkirk Tourist Information Centre (open Easter to October only)
Halliwells House, Selkirk TD7 4BL

Melrose Tourist Information Centre (open all year)
Abbey House, Abbey Street, Melrose TD6 9LG

2. Public Transport Information
Travel Line ☎ 0870 608 2608
Rail Enquiries ☎ 08457 484 950
Passenger Transport Centre, Dumfries & Galloway Council 01387 260383

3. Visit Scotland
Website: **www.visitscotland.com**
National Information and Booking Line ☎ 0845 22 55 121

4. Official website of the Southern Upland Way
www.dumgal.gov.uk/southernuplandway

5. Countryside Ranger Services
Dumfries & Galloway Council Ranger Service
Rae Street
Dumfries DG1 2JD
☎ 01387 260245 or 07702 078795 (Tom Whitty – SUW Ranger)
Email: Simon.Fieldhouse@dumgal.gov.uk

Scottish Borders Council Ranger Service
Harestanes Countryside Visitor Centre
Ancrum
Jedburgh TD8 6UQ
☎ 01835 830281
Email: mbaker@scotborders. gov.uk

6. Southern Upland Way Ltd
☎ 0870 835 8448; mobile 07747 691 447.
The Bothy, Ford House, Garroch Estate, Dalry, Castle Douglas DG7 3XP.
Website: **www.southernuplandway.com**
The website is an excellent one and includes an up-to-date accommodation list

with online booking. The website is frequently updated and includes any alterations to the SUW route. The company offers vehicle support (particularly useful to overcome the problems associated with the long section between Dalry and Sanquhar) and baggage transfer services.

7. Other commercial companies that offer vehicle backup and luggage transfer along the SUW include:

Make Tracks. 26 Forbes Road, Edinburgh EH10 4ED ☎ 0131 229 6844 **www.maketracks.net** email info@maketracks.net)
The Way Forward ☎ 01750 725 103, **www.thewayforward.org**

8. Mountain Rescue Teams covering the SUW

Galloway Mountain Rescue Team **www.gallowaymrt.org.uk**
Moffat Mountain Rescue Team **www.moffatmrt.org.uk**
Borders Rescue Team **www.bordersar.org.uk**

The relevant teams are contacted via the police on 999.

9. Taxi Services in Moffat

KY Taxis of Moffat. ☎ 01683 221481.
Moffat Taxis. ☎ 01683 221666.

10. Mountain Bothies Association (MBA)

Henderson Black & Co., Edenbridge House, 22, Crossgate, Cupar, KY15 5HW.
http://www.mountainbothies.org.uk

11. Scottish Rights of Way and Access Society

24 Annandale Street, Edinburgh EH47 4AN
www.scotways.com

NOTES

NOTES

NOTES

NOTES

NOTES

NOTES

LISTING OF CICERONE GUIDES

BACKPACKING
The End to End Trail
Three Peaks, Ten Tors
Backpacker's Britain Vol 1 –
    Northern
England
Backpacker's Britain Vol 2 – Wales
Backpacker's Britain Vol 3 –
Northern Scotland
The Book of the Bivvy

**NORTHERN ENGLAND
LONG-DISTANCE TRAILS**
The Dales Way
The Reiver's Way
The Alternative Coast to Coast
A Northern Coast to Coast Walk
The Pennine Way
Hadrian's Wall Path
The Teesdale Way

FOR COLLECTORS OF SUMMITS
The Relative Hills of Britain
Mts England & Wales Vol 2 –
    England
Mts England & Wales Vol 1 – Wales

UK GENERAL
The National Trails

BRITISH CYCLE GUIDES
The Cumbria Cycle Way
Lands End to John O'Groats – Cycle
Guide
Rural Rides No.1 – West Surrey
Rural Rides No.2 – East Surrey
South Lakeland Cycle Rides
Border Country Cycle Routes
Lancashire Cycle Way

CANOE GUIDES
Canoeist's Guide to the North-East

**LAKE DISTRICT AND
MORECAMBE BAY**
Coniston Copper Mines
Scrambles in the Lake District
    (North)
Scrambles in the Lake District
    (South)
Walks in Silverdale and
Arnside AONB
Short Walks in Lakeland 1 – South
Short Walks in Lakeland 2 – North
Short Walks in Lakeland 3 – West
The Tarns of Lakeland Vol 1 – West
The Tarns of Lakeland Vol 2 – East
The Cumbria Way &
Allerdale Ramble
Lake District Winter Climbs
Roads and Tracks of the Lake
    District
The Lake District Angler's Guide
Rocky Rambler's Wild Walks
An Atlas of the English Lakes
Tour of the Lake District
The Cumbria Coastal Way

NORTH-WEST ENGLAND
Walker's Guide to the
Lancaster Canal
Family Walks in the
Forest Of Bowland
Walks in Ribble Country
Historic Walks in Cheshire
Walking in Lancashire
Walks in Lancashire Witch Country
The Ribble Way

THE ISLE OF MAN
Walking on the Isle of Man
The Isle of Man Coastal Path
PENNINES AND

NORTH-EAST ENGLAND
Walks in the Yorkshire Dales
Walks on the North York Moors,
books 1 and 2
Walking in the South Pennines
Walking in the North Pennines
Walking in the Wolds
Waterfall Walks – Teesdale and
    High
Pennines
Walking in County Durham
Yorkshire Dales Angler's Guide
Walks in Dales Country
Historic Walks in North Yorkshire
South Pennine Walks
Walking in Northumberland
Cleveland Way and Yorkshire
Wolds
Way
The North York Moors

**DERBYSHIRE, PEAK DISTRICT,
EAST MIDLANDS**
High Peak Walks
White Peak Walks Northern Dales
White Peak Walks Southern Dales
Star Family Walks Peak District &
South Yorkshire
Walking In Peakland
Historic Walks in Derbyshire

WALES AND WELSH BORDERS
Ascent of Snowdon
Welsh Winter Climbs
Hillwalking in Wales – Vol 1
Hillwalking in Wales – Vol 2
Scrambles in Snowdonia
Hillwalking in Snowdonia
The Ridges of Snowdonia
Hereford & the Wye Valley
Walking Offa's Dyke Path
Lleyn Peninsula Coastal Path
Anglesey Coast Walks
The Shropshire Way
Spirit Paths of Wales
Glyndwr's Way
The Pembrokeshire Coastal Path
Walking in Pembrokeshire
The Shropshire Hills – A Walker's
Guide

MIDLANDS
The Cotswold Way
The Grand Union Canal Walk

Walking in Warwickshire
Walking in Worcestershire
Walking in Staffordshire
Heart of England Walks

SOUTHERN ENGLAND
Exmoor & the Quantocks
Walking in the Chilterns
Walking in Kent
Two Moors Way
Walking in Dorset
A Walker's Guide to the Isle of
Wight
Walking in Somerset
The Thames Path
Channel Island Walks
Walking in Buckinghamshire
The Isles of Scilly
Walking in Hampshire
Walking in Bedfordshire
The Lea Valley Walk
Walking in Berkshire
The Definitive Guide to
Walking in London
The Greater Ridgeway
Walking on Dartmoor
The South West Coast Path
Walking in Sussex
The North Downs Way
The South Downs Way

SCOTLAND
Scottish Glens 1 – Cairngorm Glens
Scottish Glens 2 – Atholl Glens
Scottish Glens 3 – Glens of Rannoch
Scottish Glens 4 – Glens of Trossach
Scottish Glens 5 – Glens of Argyll
Scottish Glens 6 – The Great Glen
Scottish Glens 7 – The Angus Glens
Scottish Glens 8 – Knoydart
to Morvern
Scottish Glens 9 – The Glens
of Ross-shire
The Island of Rhum
Torridon – A Walker's Guide
Walking the Galloway Hills
Border Pubs & Inns –
A Walker's Guide
Scrambles in Lochaber
Walking in the Hebrides
Central Highlands: 6 Long
Distance Walks
Walking in the Isle of Arran
Walking in the Lowther Hills
North to the Cape
The Border Country –
A Walker's Guide
Winter Climbs – Cairngorms
The Speyside Way
Winter Climbs – Ben Nevis &
Glencoe
The Isle of Skye, A Walker's Guide
The West Highland Way
Scotland's Far North
Walking the Munros Vol 1 –
Southern, Central
Walking the Munros Vol 2 –
Northern & Cairngorms
Scotland's Far West
Walking in the Cairngorms

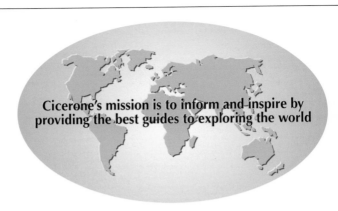

Cicerone's mission is to inform and inspire by providing the best guides to exploring the world

Since its foundation over 30 years ago, Cicerone has specialised in publishing guidebooks and has built a reputation for quality and reliability. It now publishes nearly 300 guides to the major destinations for outdoor enthusiasts, including Europe, UK and the rest of the world.

Written by leading and committed specialists, Cicerone guides are recognised as the most authoritative. They are full of information, maps and illustrations so that the user can plan and complete a successful and safe trip or expedition – be it a long face climb, a walk over Lakeland fells, an alpine traverse, a Himalayan trek or a ramble in the countryside.

With a thorough introduction to assist planning, clear diagrams, maps and colour photographs to illustrate the terrain and route, and accurate and detailed text, Cicerone guides are designed for ease of use and access to the information.

If the facts on the ground change, or there is any aspect of a guide that you think we can improve, we are always delighted to hear from you.

Cicerone Press
2 Police Square Milnthorpe Cumbria LA7 7PY
Tel:01539 562 069 Fax:01539 563 417
e-mail:info@cicerone.co.uk web:www.cicerone.co.uk